50 TALKS FOR ALL-AGE SERVICES

50 Talks
for All-Age
Services

MICHAEL BOTTING

EASTBOURNE

ISBN 0 85476 944 7

Published by
KINGSWAY COMMUNICATIONS LTD
Lottbridge Drove, Eastbourne BN23 6NT, England.
Email: books@kingsway.co.uk

Book design and production for the publishers by
Bookprint Creative Services, P.O. Box 827, BN21 3YJ, England.
Printed in Great Britain.

Contents

CONTENTS

Introduction

The primary purpose of this book is to provide help for those who are new to all-age worship. Each of the chapters suggests material for devising whole services, together with outline talks. Almost all of the talks have appeared in previous publications of mine,[1] but I have added ideas for drama, stories, hymns and prayers.

Though the word 'family' appears in all the book titles named below, the services in which the talks were used were not just for the so-called 'nuclear family' of two parents with 2.4 children, but rather for the whole church family. For that reason the title 'All-Age Services' is being used, to avoid marginalising the widowed, divorced or single parents.

As I have written in a previous book,[2] an all-age service must aim to include everyone, of whatever age, though I accept that there may have to be separate provision made for the very youngest children. It is normal in many churches these days for there to be classes for children taking place at the same time as adult morning worship. However, the material in this book is intended for those occasions when everyone above the age of five is in the main worship area. This means that the service must include items that appeal to all ages. In the next chapter I suggest ways in which this can be done.

The all-age service can also become a useful 'bridge'

---

1. Kingsway Publications: *For All the Family* (1984), *More for All the Family* (1990), *Teaching the Family* (1994), *All in the Family* (1996).
2. *All in the Family*, pages 13–21.

occasion for those adults who would like to get involved in the life of the church, but find it difficult to know how to start. An older clergyman said in my hearing some years ago that when preaching he always bore in mind that there may be some people in church for the first time, and some for the last. I try to keep that in mind, and suggest you do too. Because families who are far from any Christian commitment can be encouraged to be present, I do not think this is a suitable occasion for Holy Communion, apart from the major festivals. If you are thinking of starting all-age services I recommend that you obtain a copy of Grove Booklet 30 in the 'Evangelism' series – *Evangelising the Fringe*.[3]

Anglican readers might find it helpful to obtain a copy of the General Synod Liturgical Commission booklet *A Service of the Word*.[4] This does not provide material for all-age services, but it does outline what such services must contain to be legal.

The more people actively involved in all-age services, the better. They can read lessons, take prayers, act in dramas, accompany the singing, and so on. Further helpful guidance can also be found in *All-Age Worship* by Anne Barton.[5]

I am especially grateful to Rob Hockley, leader of the music group at St Michael's, Newton, Chester for his advice on the songs, and to Alan Stanley for his help on producing OHP acetates.

Finally, like everything else in church life, all-age worship must be supported by prayer that the Holy Spirit will guide and bless all our preparation and bring glory to our Lord Jesus Christ.

---

3. Grove Books Limited, Ridley Hall Road, Cambridge CB3 9HU.
4. Obtainable from Church House Bookshop, Great Smith Street, London SW1P 3NZ.
5. Grove Books, Worship Series 126 – see footnote 3.

Preaching at All-Age Services

Children and adults together

My initial training in speaking to all ages at once began at
Scripture Union beach missions (formerly called CSSM).
On one occasion, following my talk from a sand pulpit, a
senior officer in the RAF admitted privately to me that for
the first time he had begun to understand the meaning of the
cross of Christ. Of course, my talk had primarily been
addressed to the children.

The great German reformer, Martin Luther, said, 'A
preacher should have the skill to teach the unlearned simply,
roundly and plainly; for teaching is of more importance than
exhorting.' Then he added,

> When I preach I regard neither doctors nor magistrates, of
> whom I have above forty in the congregation. I have all my eyes
> on the servant maids and children. And if the learned men are
> not well pleased with what they hear, well, the door is open.[1]

Obviously in making our talks simple we must not go to the
extreme of reducing everything to the lowest common denom-
inator. It is part of experience to be involved sometimes in sit-
uations we cannot fully understand. Without these there would
be no real challenge or stretching in the learning process.

---

1. Quoted in Martyn Lloyd-Jones, *Preaching and Preachers* (Hodder &
Stoughton), p. 128.

To ensure that everyone feels involved, and no one feels patronised, there are certain steps that can be taken. When illustrations are used, both groups should be considered. For example, in a talk on prayer, the point might be made that we can pray at any time and in any place – at school, in the kitchen or in the office. In a longer illustration a story involving adults can be just as intelligible to children, who often watch television written primarily for adults.

Another device that can be used is to speak at different speeds. Adults can take a point being made quickly that is intended for them, whereas the children will miss it. Humorous but kindly remarks can be made at the expense of the children or the adults, which will help to maintain an informal atmosphere, as well as binding the two age groups together.

Visual aids

If you have bought this book you are probably used to reading and your only regret is that you don't have more time for it. But for a large section of the community, including the very people we want to attend our all-age services, there is a strong aversion to the printed page. They prefer a more direct, visual and sensory channel of communication. Visit your newsagent early in the day and note the piles of tabloids compared to the broadsheets. The major means of communication today are visual – television, film and the Internet. So we should make no apology for using visual aids to convey the message of our talks. I recommend Grove Booklet No.58, *Preaching for the Unchurched* by Revd Dr Roger Standing as an excellent resource.

Remember, though, that visual aids can be good servants but bad masters. First seek to ascertain the Lord's message, and then decide whether a visual aid might be used to aid the presentation of that message. Some so-called aids can actually be a hindrance both to speaker and audience, resulting in only the visual aid being remembered, and not the message. However, I for one have been provoked to see a message from the Lord through the means of visual aids, and certainly men like Jeremiah and Amos, who saw boiling pots, plumb lines and baskets of rotting summer fruit, used these images to proclaim, 'Thus says the Lord. . . .'

We need also to remember that in using visual aids we are in the perfect company of the master Teacher of all, Jesus himself. He would point to the lilies of the field, the sower, the shepherd and his flock, the fig tree, the sunset and a host of other things – using them as visual aids. Finally, he took bread and wine to illustrate the meaning of his passion.

However, there are many people who prefer radio to television because the pictures are better! Jesus was a great storyteller. In his day this was one of the main ways in which people entertained one another, and Jesus used stories to get across divine truth. The powerful stories of the Good Samaritan, and the Pharisee and publican who went to pray, create their own pictures in our minds while setting out spiritual truths. So don't feel obliged to use a visual aid. A well-told story can be very effective. But it does need to be properly rehearsed beforehand.

The most popular ways of illustrating talks are probably the overhead projector (OHP) and PowerPoint presentations. I would recommend that if you use either of these you ask someone to help you. Provide him or her with an outline of your talk, indicating where each new visual is needed. This will mean that you can have your full notes with you and concentrate on your audience.

If you use notes, prepare them on one side of the paper only, and slide them across as you go through the talk, rather than having to turn the pages over. In this way your hearers will not be so conscious that you are using notes. However, you might want to think about working without notes as often as possible. This takes a while to master, but it can be of great gain, and leaves you free to manipulate any visual aid with no lectern in the way. Provided you have prepared thoroughly beforehand, you can surely rely on the Holy Spirit to bring to your remembrance all that you have to say.

If you find it a problem to produce visual aids of adequate quality, you should not hesitate to delegate the job. There could well be people in your congregation with artistic gifts who could be persuaded to use them in the Lord's service. If such work is their normal means of livelihood you may want to consider offering payment – which should be regarded as a legitimate church expense. Give them clear directions about what you want, and adequate time to do the actual work.

Preparing your talk

All-age worship is not a subsidiary service; it is a form of worship in its own right and the talk may well need much more preparation than an 'ordinary' sermon. The late Dr Martyn Lloyd-Jones, in his helpful and entertaining book *Preaching and Preachers*,[2] speaks of struggling to get the matter of a sermon into the right divisions. I have found a hot bath can often help – and there are good medical grounds for this!

Defining your aims

When you have selected your text, subject or story, examine it thoroughly with all the normal aids you use in sermon preparation – other versions of the Bible text, commentaries and so on – so that the main teaching is grasped by you personally. It is good practice to write down in just a few words what is the main aim of the talk and what Christian doctrine you are attempting to impart. If this is difficult then you are

---

2. Hodder & Stoughton, 1971, p. 210.

probably not clear about it yourself, and your audience will not be clear either. It is better to make one point that will be remembered than several that are forgotten. Don't feel that every part of a story or parable has to be explained, or that you have to declare the 'whole counsel of God' in every talk. And do make sure you teach what the passage says and don't turn every talk into a so-called 'gospel address'.

Pay special attention to the beginning and the ending of your talk. These are the most important moments and need special care in preparation. The beginning must grab hold of your audience's attention straightaway; and the last thing you say may be the only thing they remember.

Methods of approach

The question-and-answer method

Jesus, the master Teacher, used this method in, for example, Matthew 22:41-46:

> While the Pharisees were gathered together, Jesus asked them, 'What do you think about the Christ? Whose son is he?' 'The son of David,' they replied. He said to them, 'How is it then that David, speaking by the Spirit, calls him "Lord"? For he says, "The Lord said to my Lord: 'Sit at my right hand until I put your enemies under your feet.'" If then David calls him "Lord", how can he be his son?' No-one could say a word in reply, and from that day on no-one dared to ask him any more questions.

Always make it clear to whom your questions are addressed; for example, the children. Know exactly what you are trying to draw out and word your questions carefully. Don't be too quick to answer your own questions, but keep rephrasing them until the right answer is given. If you frequently find that no one can answer your questions it may be that you need to make them simpler. A balance must be struck between appealing to the children's natural curiosity about the answer, and wearying them until they couldn't care less.

Be careful to accept answers from different children, and encourage the more timid by accepting the answers to easier questions from them. Always give credit for an attempted answer, even if it is wide of the mark. And don't think that you will always get the right answer by asking the adults!

Jesus often asked his hearers for their verdict on a story. For example, in the parable of the Good Samaritan he asks, "Which of these three was a neighbour to the man who fell into the hands of robbers?" The expert in the law replied, "The one who had mercy on him." Jesus told him, "Go and do likewise" (Luke 10:36–37).

Direct story-telling

This method can be used very well with Old Testament stories and incidents in the Gospels and the Acts. Plenty of imagination should be applied, including perhaps some anachronisms to give the stories a modern, up-to-date twist. For example, in the story of Naaman the leper, who mistakenly goes to the King of Israel for healing, you might suggest that Elisha got on his mobile to the king to tell him to send Naaman down to him! Use dramatic action – pointing at an imaginary sower, or acting the part of blind Bartimaeus calling for Jesus.

In telling any historical story you can often add greatly to your audience's interest and understanding of the story if you can show a good map. Put it on to acetate and show it on the OHP at regular intervals.

Practising this sort of talk alone beforehand can sometimes suggest improvements, and the earlier remarks about working without notes are especially applicable here.

Teaching with a visual aid

Some of Jesus' talks revolved entirely around a visual aid – a sower or a child, for example – but we need to take care that our points are not forced, and that there is clear biblical backing for the points we are making.

Writing your talk

When your text, aim and method have all been decided upon, you need to set down an outline of the talk. When you first begin you might want to write out every word, ensuring that the talk follows a logical sequence and that every illustration has been thought through. As mentioned above, spend time getting the beginning right, and you might want to make a definite point about two-thirds of the way through the talk, when interest might be flagging. A good illustration or visual aid at that point may help to bring the talk to a successful conclusion.

If you are new to giving such talks, you might want to start this book by looking at Talks 10, 24 and 41, where I have expanded the notes somewhat to be of help.

Final note

Having said that the most popular ways of illustrating talks are by means of OHP or PowerPoint, I would like to add that a number of talks in this book are based on the assumption that a Teazlegraph board is available. I still think that the Teazlegraph has a lot going for it, but the method could be adapted to OHP if necessary.

Teazlegraph was a trade name for material that could be used to cover a large board. Velcro is then attached to the back of words or pictures so that they can be stuck onto the board. The firm who made the material has now gone out of business, but a similar effect can be achieved with nylon velvet. Use a dark colour, such as navy blue, and choose something with a foam backing for extra durability. Use the material to cover a plywood board about 5' by 4', sticking it with Evostick or Uhu. Make strips of cardboard of varying lengths and about 5″ wide and cover these with nylon velvet in the same way. These can be used for letters and words. Attach Velcro to the back of the strips, and any pictures that you are using, with strong glue.

Good lettering is worth a lot of trouble. As a basic principle, 4″ lettering should be used, mostly in lower case. Cut letters from fluorescent poster card, which can be obtained in several colours from art shops. Each letter should have two small Velcro squares stuck on the back. Words can be made up on your cardboard strips and attached to the main board at appropriate moments in the talk.

For an ideal board cover both sides with nylon velvet. Mount it on a heavy-duty mild steel tripod, with a central column containing a ball-race at the top and bottom. A mild steel rod screws into the central column and the 5' by 4' board is then mounted on the rotating rod giving the two pictures surfaces. A member of the congregation of my first parish with engineering skills made my stand. A friend of mine had his made by a small local engineering firm after explaining his requirements. Alternatively, hook-and-loop display boards can be purchased via www.ultralon.co.uk

Producing OHP Acetates

Getting started

Obviously you will need access to a computer. The word processing program will enable you to produce words that can be copied onto acetates for use on the OHP. You can change the size of the lettering, the font (ie, typeface) and the colour, if you have a colour printer. Coloured acetates make a much greater impact than monochrome, though you should avoid weak colours such as yellow.

Use a font that is clear, bold and not too formal, such as Comic Sans or Arial. You may be able to enhance your lettering, for example by 'engraving'. Look at the format section of your program and see what is available under the font heading.

You may be giving a talk which has four key words each beginning with the same letter. You could use a larger size and different colour for the first letter of each word and engrave it for greater impact.

Experiment by printing onto paper. Make sure the lettering is large enough to be seen from the back of the church. Try to plan the printing to make the most use of each sheet of acetate, even if this means some cutting out. Buy some acetate sheets designed for colour printing and print directly onto the film. It is much cheaper to buy special film than visit your local colour copy shop and have them copy onto acetates for you.

Moving on

From producing coloured words it is only a short step to producing coloured pictures. These can be obtained from three main sources.

Clip art files

Most congregations will have someone who has a computer that contains a clip art file. If not there may be someone on the edge of your fellowship who is just waiting for a way in. The 'Church Leadership Pack' by CPAS contains clip art suitable for each season on CD-ROM. Other Christian clip art collections are:

Sunrise Softwear, PO Box 19, Carlisle CA3 OHP
Tel: 0845 0579579
Website: www.sunrise-software.com
Email: Sales@sunrise-softwear.com

Christian Computer Art, 33 Bramley Way, Hardwick, Cambridge CB3 7XD
Tel: 01954 2100097
Website: www.cc-art.com
Email: Tech@cc-art.com

McCrimmon Publishing Co Ltd, 10–12 High Street, Great Wakering, Essex SS3 OEQ
Email: mccrimmons@dial.pipex.com

More general clip art can be obtained from Microsoft Publisher and Desktop Publishing. Having chosen your clip art, print on acetates in colour.

Existing pictures

You may have a collection of pictures that can be scanned into a computer. Flat-bed scanners are found in many computer packages. If you do not have access to one the cost is relatively modest and a congregation may feel it is a worthwhile investment. Subject to any copyright restrictions pictures from, for example, children's Bibles may be scanned into the computer and then printed in colour onto acetate. Similarly the line drawings produced by many publishers to help Sunday school teachers can be scanned and printed on acetate. These can later be hand coloured if needed, perhaps by someone in the congregation with artistic talent.

Using this technique you could ask them to produce a series of small pictures which, when scanned and reproduced on acetate, will have the same effect as a picture the size of your projection screen.

Specially produced pictures

Should there be someone in the congregation with a digital camera your imagination may be the only limit to the visual aids you can produce. Just as Jesus used local events in his parables, you may be able to illustrate your talk with something similar. A talk on healing, for example, could contain a local hospital, a local GP's surgery, a nurse, and a minister praying for healing in your church.

Almost professional!

The next step is a little bigger. It involves editing the clip art images. A talk may require the display of a number of boxes of chocolates for instance. By selecting a picture of a box of chocolates from the clip art, and using the DTP program, it is possible to add appropriate lettering to the boxes. If one of the boxes is available when you want to do the talk, you can also use a flat-bed scanner to scan the box front into the publishing program and then print in colour onto acetate.

The techniques for using Desk Top Publishing vary with

the program. Most are easily mastered. If you need help
there may well be people in the congregation, especially from
a young people's group, only too pleased to provide it. Just
ask!

Alan Stanley, Leeds
Michael Botting, Chester

Notes on Source Material

Texts

Where longer passages are being read aloud, *The Dramatised Bible* (edited by Michael Perry, published by Marshall Pickering / Bible Society) is especially recommended.

Drama

Various publications are available, but I have used: *50 Sketches for All Occasions*, edited by Michael Botting (Kingsway); *Acting Up* by Dave Hopwood and *Scenes and Wonders* by Paul Powell (both published by Church House Publishing).

When any of this material is used in public the source, author and publisher should be made known. Before considering using material from any of the above publications, the conditions on performing rights and photocopying should be read and complied with. Permission is generally given free of charge for performances before live, non-paying audiences.

Stories

A number of stories from the author's own experience are included in these talks. If you cannot think of a story of your own to illustrate the point then you could perhaps introduce the printed story with the words 'I once heard of . . .'.

Hymns and songs

Suggestions for songs and hymns are from *Songs of Fellowship* (Kingsway Music, Eastbourne), or *Hymns for Today's Church* (Hodder & Stoughton).

Prayers

Suggestions for prayers are taken from *400 Prayers for Church, Home and School*, formerly entitled *Prayers for All the Family* by Michael Botting (Kingsway); and from *Common Worship* (Church House Publishing).

THE CHRISTIAN YEAR

1. Ready for Christ's Return?

Aim

To make three important points about the Second Coming of Christ and especially that we must be awake and ready for him.

Texts

Romans 13:8–14 (which could be read as the Lesson); 1 Thessalonians 4:16–5:6 (which should be read during the talk as indicated).

Drama

Interview with St Augustine of Hippo (see outline below).

Hymns and songs

'Awake, awake, O Zion' (SOF 35); 'Great is the darkness' (SOF 742); 'Lo, He comes with clouds descending' (SOF 347); 'We have sung our songs of victory' (SOF 1092).

Prayers

400 Prayers 6, 7, 257, 357.

Main talk

Preparation

Prepare an OHP acetate, the top part having the words JESUS WILL RETURN AGAIN TO THIS WORLD and underneath Jesus depicted coming in glory with two angels on either side of him blowing trumpets.

On the middle to lower part have a piece of acetate to flip over, being attached by Sellotape to one side of the main acetate. On this have the words WE CANNOT KNOW WHEN and a conventional picture of a burglar with mask and swag bag, getting into a house to the right of the words.

At the very bottom have a strip of acetate to flip over with the words WE MUST KEEP AWAKE AND BE READY.

Have a second acetate with a picture of a man in night-clothes, unshaven, with tousled hair, answering a front door.

Have a person dressed in pyjamas, dressing-gown and slippers concealed, but ready to come into church when called. Have his suit concealed near where the talk is being given. Have another person dressed in a white flowing robe depicting St Augustine of Hippo, who should also be concealed until his interview.

This talk can either be given all in one piece, or form part of an Advent family carol service with the three points being given as separate talks.

Presentation

Ask what time of year it is in the church's calendar. Elicit the answer 'Advent' and ask what that means and whose coming we are expecting. Clearly distinguish between Jesus' first and second coming and stress that we are thinking about the second, which we say we believe in when we say the Creed.

Proceed to make the following three main points:

1. *Jesus will return again to this world.* (Show the top half of OHP acetate.) Explain that the very early Christians, especially those living in Thessalonica, were very upset that their friends were dying and Jesus had not yet returned to the world. The apostle Paul wrote to them about Jesus' return. Read 1 Thessalonians 4:16–17. Contrast this with Jesus' first coming.

2. *We cannot know when Jesus will return.* (Flip over middle part of OHP acetate.) Read 1 Thessalonians 5:1–4. Explain that very unfortunately burglars never give advance warning of their arrival! Burglars may come at any time – day or night. Though we know they may come, we are still taken by surprise when they do. The same will be true of the Lord Jesus. Perhaps explain that a gunner in an artillery battery knows all the signs of when a gun is about to be fired, yet he still 'jumps' when it goes off. If time allows explain that Jesus, when on earth, did not know the time of his return (Matthew 24:36), so we should never take seriously anyone who attempts to tell us exactly when he is going to return.

3. *We must keep awake and be ready.* (Flip over the last piece of acetate.) Read 1 Thessalonians 5:5–6. Ask if anyone thinks they have heard something similar to those verses this morning. So direct the congregation back to Romans 13:8–14.

Refer to the different clothes we wear and their significance, eg Guides and Scouts, clerical collars. Proceed to point out that there is appropriate clothing for day and for night. At this point the person in night-clothes enters and walks up the main aisle of the church. Refer to the fact that although we were all happily wearing such clothes at 3.00 am, most of us are not wearing these clothes now. Point out that although we can only see one person in night-clothes, when God looks on us as a church he may see many of us in night-clothes. Refer to Romans 13:11–12.

Ask the person who is wearing night-clothes to attempt to put on his suit (which you have brought out of hiding) on top of his night-clothes. Mention that everyone will see the impossibility and pointlessness of the exercise. But this is what most of us attempt to do spiritually. The Bible tells us first to *cast off* the deeds of darkness, and then to *put on* the Lord Jesus Christ and all that means.

Ask St Augustine of Hippo to join you and proceed to interview him as follows:

Interviewer: Augustine, thank you for granting us this unique interview. I understand you were not the only famous Augustine in the history of the church.

Augustine: That's correct. I have a famous namesake who lived about 250 years after me and became the first Archbishop of Canterbury in about 600 AD.

I: But you also became a bishop?

A: Yes, I eventually became Bishop of Hippo, in North Africa.

I: Where were you born?

A: In North Africa, in a country you would call Algeria today.

I: Were you brought up in a Christian home?

A: My mother, Monica, was a very devout Christian. From my earliest days she taught me about Jesus and what it meant to follow him. I was due to be baptised, but I had many questions and doubts and so my baptism was delayed. However, I had a very good education. I loved studying the great writers and speakers of my day. For a time I was a lecturer.

I: But you obviously became a Christian eventually. How did that happen?

A: I was seriously searching for the truth, but at the same time there were lots of temptations, as there always are, and I was led into evil ways. I felt I was enslaved by my sins. One day I was weeping and crying to God, and was very sorry about the state of my life, when I heard the voice of a child in a nearby house singing. It kept on repeating a chorus, 'Take it and read, take it and read.' To begin with I took no notice, but then I wondered if God was speaking to me through this child. I stopped crying and thought that God was commanding me to open my book of Scripture and read the first passage on which my eyes fell.

I: So what did you do?

A: I hurried back to where I had been reading a book containing the letters of St Paul. I seized it and opened it and in silence read the first passage I saw, which was in Romans chapter 13: 'Let us behave decently, as in the daytime, not in orgies and drunkenness, not in sexual immorality and debauchery, not in dissension and jealousy. Rather, clothe yourselves with the Lord Jesus Christ, and do not think about how to gratify the desires of the sinful nature.' I had no need to read more. In an instant it was as though the light of faith had flooded into my life and all the darkness and doubt was dispelled.

I: Then what did you do?

A: I shared what had happened with a friend, and, of course, very especially with my mother, who was overjoyed to see her many prayers for me answered.

I: Thank you so much for sharing your remarkable story with us.

Ask the congregation, 'Are you ready for the return of Jesus?'

Show the second acetate and refer to the passage, 'The night is nearly over; the day is almost here. So let us put aside the deeds of darkness and put on the armour of light.'

Will Jesus catch us still in our night-clothes when he returns?

[Note: The earlier part of this talk is based on one by Michael Botting appearing in the Scripture Union magazine *Learning All Together*, January–March 1993. The latter part was suggested by the Revd Peter Markby, Lewes, Sussex.]

2. Christmas Good Newspaper

Aim

To provide a Christmas Day newspaper on the day when there are no secular newspapers, but unlike them yours is only concerned with good news.

Text

Luke 2:10–11.

Drama

50 Sketches for All Occasions 4 'The Reluctant Shepherd'.

Hymns and songs

'Immanuel, O Immanuel' (SOF 233); 'Good news, good news to you we bring' (SOF 739); 'The virgin Mary had a baby boy' (SOF 1050); 'While shepherds watched their flocks by night' (HTC 94).

Prayers

400 Prayers 12–14, 258–260.

Main talk

Preparation

Design a sheet of cardboard to look like the front page of a newspaper. I used the title BETHLEHEM (in roman type four inches high), followed by a red painted star, and a main heading in black: *BABY BORN IN A STABLE*. Cut out of the card four rectangles, and place behind them in the gaps, paper in different colours with the words:

Good News   *A Saviour*   *great joy*   *to all people*

Then pass nylon thread through the main card and the four rectangles you have cut out, as described in Talk 4 on page 40.

Presentation

Point out that there are no newspapers on Christmas Day, but that you have brought one to make up for it, but unlike most newspapers this one is only concerned with *good news* (move down first card). The very news that the angel brought to the shepherds at the first Christmas time (quote text).

1. *A message of great joy* (move down third card). Quote 'Behold I bring you good tidings of great joy'. Elaborate on the joy that the coming of a baby brings. Perhaps mention a recent famous birth, say to Victoria and David Beckham. When God's Son came it was a time of great joy. Christmas should therefore be a time of great joy with special events planned. But why only at Christmas? The Christmas message is always true and Christians should have the joy of Christmas in their hearts throughout the year.

2. *A message to all people* (move down bottom card). Quote verse 10. The news of a new baby in the home quickly

travels. When the Queen's son, Charles, was born there were news flashes on television, and radio programmes were interrupted. The foreign office were informing embassies throughout the world. At the birth of God's Son the news was sent to rich and poor; to wise men by a star, to shepherds by angels; to Jew and Gentile, for the shepherds would have been local Jews, and the wise men Gentiles from the East. Before Jesus ascended back to his Father in heaven, he told the disciples to 'Go tell all nations'. William Temple once said, 'If the Christian gospel is true for anyone anywhere, it is true for everyone everywhere.' So it is a message for you: John, Mary, Uncle George, Aunt Matilda, Mummy, Daddy, Grandma. Why?

3. *A message about a Saviour* (lower second card). Quote verse 11. One of the first questions when the baby arrives is 'Is it a boy or a girl?' And then, 'What's it going to be called?'

When John Snagge announced the birth of the Queen's son in 1948 he said, 'The Queen has had her baby – it's a boy.' The name (Charles) was announced some time later. But when God's Son was born things were rather different. (i) Mary knew her baby was going to be a boy. (ii) The name had been given to her – Jesus means Saviour (Matthew 1:21). Why was this so important? Enlarge on all people being sinners, and needing a Saviour.

4. *Conclusion*. I wonder if you have really received the 'good news' of Christmas? It is because we are all sinners that we need to hear the message about the Saviour. It is only those who have received the message of the Saviour who know that it is a message of great joy.

3. God's Christmas Card

Aim

To tell the Christmas story using a fairly elaborate visual aid. The talk is suitable for a Christmas tree or Christingle service.

Text

Luke 2:11–12.

Drama

Details included in the talk below.

Hymns and songs

Carols that include references to cradle, cross and crown. Also 'Jesus the Name above all names' (SOF 306); 'The light of Christ' (SOF 1026); 'Like a candle flame' (SOF 891).

Prayers

400 Prayers 12–14, 258–260.

Main talk

Preparation

Design a large Christmas card, say 5′ by 3′4″ or 1.5m × 1m (white card can be purchased from good stationery wholesalers in this size). You'll need two sheets. It is essential if the card is to stand up that it has a wooden frame around its sides and that the join has proper hinges. The inside of the card should show at the top in black script 'To all sinners'. Below it in brightly coloured script put 'Happy Christmas'. The outside of the card could be covered with an attractive Christmas wrapping-paper pasted down. In the lower part cut out a large circular hole 2'9" or 83.5 cm in diameter, the bottom of the hole being about 7.5" or 19 cm from the bottom of the card. When the card is semi-closed, the wording 'Happy Christmas' inside the card should be fully visible through the hole. In the top part of the outside of the card cut out shapes of a cradle to the left, a cross central, and a crown to the right. Coloured day-glo paper – yellow, red and orange respectively – should be stuck over the gaps and the shapes of the cradle, cross and crown fitted back into the card, so that they are not evident at the beginning of the talk.

Arrange to have four responsible children dressed up as Mary, Joseph, a shepherd and a king. Provide the shepherd with a fleece. Have a small manger with hay or straw and possibly a light in it that can be lit at the appropriate moment. The four children and the manger should be somewhere close to where the talk is being given, but out of sight. There should be an angle-poise lamp near where the card will be placed, which can later be switched on to light up the inside of the card. Obtain from the Post Office a postman's outfit. I have never had any problem in borrowing one, but you will not be able to borrow a badge, so one will need to be made out of cardboard. Dress up a suitable man who will fit the uniform and ask him to wait outside the room or church where the talk is to be given.

Presentation

Explain the problem a friend of yours had one Christmas when he was handed two Christmas cards to deliver to God and Jesus. Of course, Christmas is a celebration of Jesus' birthday, but it is more about a message from God to us than us to God, so we are going to think about God's Christmas card to us. Explain that every Christmas card must have:

1. *A sender* Ask why we send cards. Suggest: because we have always done so; because some people would be offended if we didn't; because we love the person. Agree that the last is the reason why God has sent a message to us: because he loves us.

2. *A deliverer* Ask how most cards come to us, and on receiving the reply 'By the postman' ask your postman to come in with the card. Discover to whom it is addressed, and on seeing 'To all sinners', ask who that means. Enlarge on the problem of sin in the world, but stress that we are all to blame. The card should be placed slightly open, so that the words 'Happy Christmas' are lit by the angle-poise lamp and can be seen by all.

3. *The message* It is all about Jesus:
    (a) *The cradle*. Perhaps explain the problem of making a pet understand what you are saying. You really need to become a dog, so that you can bark the same language! At Christmas God became a man, so that he could speak to us person to person. The holy family should come out from the card through the hole, bringing the manger, which should then be lit up. Take the cradle shape from the top of the outside of the card, which will show up because of the light from the angle-poise lamp.
    (b) *The cross*. Explain that Jesus came to be more than just a man. Refer to the message of the angels to the shepherds, stressing the word 'Saviour'. The shepherd could come through the card carrying his fleece. Point out that sheep have more than one use. They give us wool, but also

something else. Enquire what, and on receiving the answer that they provide lamb or mutton to eat, explain that that means they have to die. Explain that Jesus had to die to be our Saviour, and take out the cross shape from the top of the outside of the card.

(c) *The crown.* Ask who else came to visit the baby Jesus, and on receiving an answer about kings, the king enters through the card. Explain that Jesus did more than die. He also rose from the dead and ascended to his Father in heaven, where he now reigns. He calls us to make him both Saviour and King of our lives. Take out the crown shape from the top of the outside of the card.

4. *The receiver* When the postman comes, we don't have to receive our cards. We probably all know someone who's had a card returned! But have we received God's message: the offer of a Saviour and a King?

Postscript

Ask the postman how we know he is one. He shows his badge: that witnesses to his being a real postman. If we have received God's message, we should also be like postmen – delivering the message everywhere (see Acts 1:8).

4. God's Christmas Gift

Aim

To present the message of Christmas by means of a Christmas parcel.

Text

2 Corinthians 9:15.

Drama

Scenes and Wonders 'The Shepherds' Christmas', pp. 45–49.

Hymns and songs

Carols referring to Jesus as God's gift, eg 'O little town of Bethlehem' (SOF 420). Also his suffering to bring us salvation, eg 'From heaven You came' (SOF 120).

Prayers

400 Prayers 12–14, 258–260.

Main talk

Preparation

Cover a large piece of cardboard 3′4″ by 2′4″ with attractive Christmas paper. Cut out some rectangular sections of the cardboard 4½" wide and about 3' long. In the gaps stick behind your parcel black cardboard or paper and, using letters cut out of fluorescent paper stuck onto the black, the following words: 'What we want', 'Free to us', 'Costly to God'. In the word 'Costly' make the 'T' like a cross. Fix the rectangular pieces of cardboard back in the following way.

Obtain a good length of very thin nylon thread. This can be obtained from a shop selling angling equipment. Make some holes in your cardboard, knot the thread at one end and thread about ½" above the first gap. Bring the thread through the rectangle that has been cut out, about 1" top and bottom, and then thread it about 1" from the next rectangle. Proceed as illustrated. When the whole visual aid has been threaded the effect will be that the pieces cut out can be raised and lowered and yet still remain part of the visual aid. On a separate piece of black card put the letters of *Jesus* and have a slot above your present where *Jesus* can be fitted. Finally, put a piece of ribbon right round your gift with a coloured tag on it: 'To everyone, with love from God, 2 Corinthians 9:15'.

Presentation

Speak about the special feature of Christmas being the giving of presents. Refer to the Wise Men from the East with their gifts. Reveal the visual aid and refer to the label. Ask what God's special gift at Christmas time is and then refer to Jesus as God's inexpressible (or use AV's 'unspeakable') gift, quoting the text.

Many will celebrate Christmas without a thought for God's gift. The Bible says we should thank God for his great gift of the Lord Jesus. Why? Remove the ribbon from your parcel, fix the word 'Jesus' above it and in turn reveal three reasons why Jesus is the ideal gift at Christmas.

1. *What we want* Many people on receiving a Christmas present say, 'That is just what I wanted,' and although it is

questionable whether this is always true, it is certainly true of
Jesus, for we are all sinners and he came into the world to be
our Saviour. 'There was no other good enough to pay the
price of sin; he *only* could unlock the gate of heaven and let
us in.' Unfortunately, many people do not seem to *want*
Jesus; we all *need* him, but it may be only later that we realise
that we want him.

2. *Free to us* One of the essential things about a gift is that
it is free. Enlarge on the fact that we cannot earn our salvation. If God's gift were not free we would all be lost.

3. *Costly to God* The reason why Jesus is free to us is because
of what it cost God to give him. Point out the cross on the
word 'Costly' and enlarge on the cost. Reference could be
made to the story of Abraham and his son. But God did not
spare his Son. When we realise what it cost God to give us
his great Christmas gift we should want to receive the Lord
Jesus Christ (John 1:12–13) and to say 'Thanks be to God
for his inexpressible gift.'

5. Christmas Tree Lights

Aim

To show what it means to be a Christian by way of a topical Christmas visual aid.

Text

Philippians 2:14–15.

Hymns and songs

Carols that make some reference to light, eg 'Angels from the realms of glory' (HTC 77); 'Come and sing the Christmas story' (HTC 81); 'The Light of Christ' (SOF 1026); 'O little town of Bethlehem' (SOF 420).

Prayers

400 Prayers 12–14, 258–260.

Main talk

Preparation

On cardboard draw the outline of a Christmas tree, which should be at least 32″ high and appear to come out of a brightly coloured pot. Put a star at the top of the tree. Divide the space of the tree into eight sections 4″ high, and write on the alternate spaces the words 'wor-', 'world',

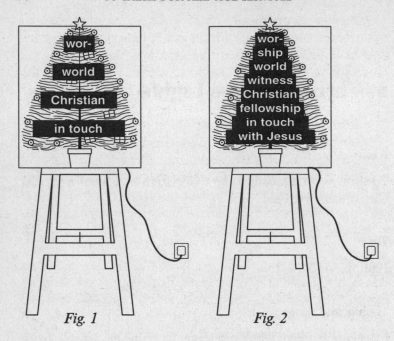

Fig. 1   *Fig. 2*

'Christian', 'in touch', on a black background, as in figure 1. Cover these spaces with slightly longer rectangular pieces of card, and then paint the Christmas tree, sticking on pieces of coloured fluorescent paper to represent parcels. Fold all the cards down and write on them, on a black background, the words 'ship', 'witness', 'fellowship', 'with Jesus', so that the finished tree appears as in figure 2. The letters are more effective if cut out of fluorescent paper and stuck on. Around the tree fix a set of Christmas tree lights. Begin the talk with the cards folded up so that no words can be seen.

Presentation

What is the first thing you notice about a Christmas tree? Answer: lights. The Bible compares Christians to lights. Read text and explain.

1. *Christians are in touch with Jesus* Christmas tree needs to be switched on or plugged in before it lights up. Christians also need to be in touch with Christ and the power of his Holy Spirit. (Turn down the bottom card.) Enlarge on the need for repentance and faith and switch on the lights.

2. *Christian fellowship* Once we are in touch with Christ we become part of his church. This means that we have to work together. (Turn down the next card.) We are dependent on each other. Most of you will know that if you unscrew one of these lights all the rest go out (do so to illustrate). And when one Christian is not pulling his or her weight in the fellowship all the others are affected.

3. *World witness* We especially notice a Christmas tree when it is lit up. The text tells us that Christians are to 'shine as lights in the world'. (Turn down the next card.) We must be seen, and seen to be different. This should show by the life we lead and by the words we say.

4. *Worship* When you see a lovely Christmas tree do you say, 'What wonderful lights'? No, you say, 'What a wonderful Christmas tree,' and we must so live to glorify God that when people see us they do not say 'What wonderful people,' but 'What a wonderful God we worship.' (Turn down the top card.)

6. Three Trees

Aim

To state the essentials of the gospel by linking up three references to trees in the Bible.

Texts

Genesis 2:9; 1 Peter 2:24; Revelation 22:2.

Drama

50 Sketches for All Occasions 7 'The Passion'; 8 'Nailed!'; 9 'Heaven's Above'.

Hymns and songs

Possibly the carol 'The holly and the ivy'; 'Jesus, we celebrate your victory' (SOF 309).

Prayers

400 Prayers 2, 36, 38, 39, 66, 196, 248, 251, 383.

Main talk

Preparation

Draw the outline of a Christmas tree exactly symmetrically. Cut out another tree of similar shape; divide it exactly down

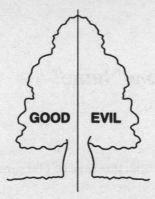

the middle. Place second tree on top of the first and by means of sellotape or white plaster fix the tree so that it can be folded over to reveal three different trees, as illustrated.

The first tree should look more or less like a tree but have the words *Good* and *Evil* marked on either side. The second tree should be red with a black cross painted in the middle. The third should be gold.

Presentation

1. *Good and evil* Refer to Genesis 2:9 and tell briefly the story of the Garden of Eden and its trees and how Adam and Eve chose evil and were turned out of the garden. How could they ever come back and resume fellowship with God?

2. *Refer to the cross* (called a 'tree') and what Jesus did on it.

3. *The tree of life* Refer back to Genesis 3:22 and now to Revelation 2:7 and 22:2 and speak briefly about heaven.

7. What's in a Name?

Aim

To explain the essential message of Christmas using a simple visual aid.

Text

Matthew 1:21.

Drama

Acting Up 'Nativity Scene', p. 46

Hymns and songs

Christmas section of hymn book, especially 'Good Christians all, rejoice' ('Good Christian men rejoice' HTC 85); 'Jesus, good above all other' (HTC 96); 'Jesus, Name above all names' (SOF 306).

Prayers

400 Prayers 12–14, 258–260.

Main talk

Preparation

Prepare two cards, one with 'Your name' on one side and 'Sinner' on the reverse. The other card has 'Saviour' on one side and 'Jesus' on the reverse. Have either a clean blackboard with some white chalk, or an OHP acetate and marker. Have a red cloth available.

Presentation

Ask people how many of them know the meaning of their names and produce the card with 'Your name' on it. Mention, for example, that 'Matthew' means 'gift of God', 'Claire', 'bright', etc. Most of us don't know, or care, about the meaning of our names, but this was not so in Bible times. 'Peter' means 'a rock'; 'Boanerges' means 'sons of thunder' and Jesus made reference to both. However, there is a name we all have in common, a name that really describes us all. Ask for suggestions and accept the answer 'Sinner'. Turn your card round. Perhaps some of us feel we have not lived very bad lives. Enlarge on the number of sins we have committed since we were born. This may be illustrated as follows. All of us have sinned many times a day but supposing, on average, we had only sinned three times a day. Then how many sins would we have committed in a year? Go on questioning and write the following on your blackboard or OHP acetate:

For a ten-year-old $365 \times 10 \times 3 = 10,950$
plus leap years, say 2, $\underline{6}$
$10,956$ sins

For a 40-year-old $43,800$
plus leap years, say 10, $\underline{30}$
$43,830$ sins

So sin is more serious than perhaps we thought. Elaborate on the results of sin in everyday life, such as those caused by drunken driving. But, far more seriously, sin separates us from God. Produce other card with the name 'Jesus' showing. Ask why the Lord Jesus was given this name. Who knows what his name means? Turn to Matthew 1:21 and quote, drawing out 'Saviour' as the answer to the question, turning round card to show 'Saviour' on back. Comment that Jesus lived a sinless life, otherwise he could not save sinners. He died on the cross and shed his blood for us. He rose from death to prove he is our living Saviour. His blood alone can blot out our sins. Refer to Isaiah 44:22 and 1 John 1:7. Then wipe the blackboard or OHP acetate clean with the red cloth.

End by asking whom Jesus saves and draw people's attention to 'his people'. In other words he saves those who belong to him. Ask whether everyone has given their lives to Jesus-Saviour?

8. The Gifts of the Wise Men

Aim

To explain the significance of the wise men's gifts.

Text

Matthew 2:11.

Drama

Scenes and Wonders 'The Shepherds' Christmas', pp. 45–49.

Hymns and songs

Christmas carols that mention the gifts of the wise men: 'The first nowell'; 'As with gladness'; 'Wise men, they came to look for wisdom' (HTC 93, 99, 100); 'I will offer up my life' (SOF 851).

Prayers

400 Prayers 16, 17, 262, 361.

Main talk

Preparation

Can be told without visual aids, but can be very effective based round an enlarged Christmas stocking or Christmas cracker. Gifts with the words *gold*, etc. marked on them are produced out of the stocking or cracker. If the cracker idea (or even three crackers) is used, the bang can be made with a toy gun that fires caps. This also ensures the congregation is kept alert!

Presentation

Enquire if any members of the congregation hangs up stockings at Christmas. Recap the story of the wise men bringing presents to the baby Jesus.

1. *Meaningful gifts* If someone received a lot of soap for Christmas they might say, 'Is someone trying to tell me something?' All the wise men's gifts tell us something important about Jesus. Enlarge on each:

• Gold – tribute for a King
• Frankincense – worship for God
• Myrrh – balm for one who died

2. *Wonderful gifts* Explain that these gifts were very costly, quite apart from all the time and trouble taken to get them to their destination. Tell a story of a child who brought a broken toy to a toy service; it had not cost much. If this talk is given in a toy service, express the hope that no broken toy was given today.

The wise men brought such costly gifts because of who Jesus was. The greatest gift we can give Jesus is our lives, and he especially wants us while we are young. Refer to D. L. Moody's observation that twelve-and-a-half lives were given to Christ at one of his meetings, ie twelve children and one adult.

3. *Useful gifts* Explain that we would not expect our fathers to be given handbags for Christmas, or our mothers after-

shave. The wise men's gifts were very useful for the holy family's trip to Egypt: gold to use as money, frankincense to keep away flies and make the home smell nice, myrrh would be excellent baby powder. If we want our lives to be really useful we must put them into the hands of Jesus.

Perhaps end with the story of Victor Trumper, the cricketer who once scored a century with a child's bat. The secret was that the little bat was in the hands of the master player.

9. A Talk for Lent or Gift Day

Aim

To stimulate concern and generosity for the third world and for helping charitable organisations like TEAR Fund.

Text

John 6:1–14.

Drama

The talk itself is dramatic in the use of the family.

Hymns and songs

'I'll praise my Maker while I've breath' (HTC 20); 'Son of God, eternal Saviour' (HTC 317); 'Forty days and forty nights' (HTC 102); 'When Jesus walked upon this earth' (HTC 324); 'God of grace and God of glory' (HTC 103); 'Judge eternal, throned in splendour' (HTC 329); 'Break Thou the Bread of Life' (SOF 50); 'O Lord, the clouds are gathering' (SOF 429).

Prayers

400 Prayers 94, 174, 175, 274, 301, 403.

Main talk

Preparation

Obtain the assistance of a church family and the equipment named in the presentation. Perhaps have an OHP or teazle-graph board for the main headings of the talk and the sub-headings under 'Secret of the child' (see below).

Presentation

Introduce the talk by mentioning picnics (with special reference to any church picnics you may have had where the crowd was quite large). Refer to what must have been one of the largest picnics in history and describe the feeding of the five thousand – which may only have been the number of men.

1. *Size of the crowd* Consider the problem of feeding such a large number following on from Jesus' discussion with Philip. Mention the very much greater problem of feeding about 2,000 million very hungry people in the world today. But it is not just food they need. Let's take a typical Western family.

The pre-arranged family come and sit on comfortable chairs in front of the congregation. Nearby are tables carrying the various items to be taken away from them.

- *Food*. Take away tinned food and cake. Leave some potatoes and beans.
- *Clothing*. Take away all outer clothing. Leave shoes on the man only.
- *Home*. Remove door (made of cardboard), chairs, tables and TV. Leave a blanket.
- *Schooling*. Remove all books.
- *Public services*. Remove telephone handset or mobile, bottles of medicine. Leave a very old bicycle.
- *Money*. Allow £2.

Ask the congregation what to do. Do we send them away? Jesus said to his disciples 'You give them something to eat.'

2. *Smallness of the contribution* (Refer to v.9.) Explain that the barley loaves would be poor man's food and fish probably no more than a pickled relish. The lad would only be a small boy who would not carry much. Then describe what Jesus did and the enormous supply of food there was, as implied in verses 11–13.

Go on to explain that compared to the needs of the world we ourselves have little to offer, like the lad, but as St Augustine put it, 'Without God we cannot, without us God will not.'

3. *Secret of the child*

- *He gave his small contribution to Jesus.* That was all, but little becomes much when God is involved. Supremely God wants not our money, but us.
- *He gave all his contribution to Jesus.* He held nothing back. Refer to the widow's mite and the story of Ananias and Sapphira. God knows how much we give and how much we withhold. He does not ask of us more than he was prepared to give. He so loved that he gave Jesus.
- *He did not go without himself.* All were filled, which must have included the lad. Whether it be our money, possessions or our whole lives we shall never lose by giving to God's work, but rather lose if we do not give.

End with a suitable story or mention the testimony of tithers, who, once they start, never give the practice up.

10. Mothering Sunday

Aim

The talk is suitable for various occasions, but especially for Mothering Sunday (fourth in Lent), where it is designed to be non-threatening to those who are single, divorced or widowed.

The occasion when I first gave it was to be my last at St Matthew's, Fulham, and was to include the baptism of the grandson of my former secretary and her husband, one of my churchwardens. This rather special occasion had been in my prayers for some time when I came across a delightful illustration about family life based on the family at Bethany where Jesus spent many happy hours. It was not long before the outline took shape as described in the Preparation below.

Text

John 12:1–8. See also Luke 10: 38–42.

Hymns and songs

'Father God, I wonder' (SOF 92); 'Jesus put this song into our hearts' (SOF 299); 'What a Friend I've found' (SOF 1109).

Prayers

400 Prayers 68, 96, 111 (litany), 131, 199, 230, 236, 244, 283–287.

Main talk

Preparation

The Christian family

Lazarus	Witness	Home
Martha	Worker	Hands
Mary	Worshipper	Heart

An artist in my congregation drew me some delightful figures on white card of Lazarus and his two sisters. She also painted some hands on pink fluorescent paper which I cut out. I drew and cut out a house on orange fluorescent paper and a heart on red fluorescent paper. From my arsenal of Teazlegraph letters I put on Teazlegraph strips the three words *Witness*, *Worker*, and *Worshipper*. I stuck Velcro on the back of all the figures and the Teazlegraph strips. (The words *The Christian Family* can also be put on the Teazlegraph board.) Appropriate adaptions will have to be made if using an OHP.

Presentation

What is different about the Christian family? The Bible has much to say about family life and the upbringing of children. (I enlarged on this point.) Jesus knew all about family life: the problem of helping out when Joseph had died, brothers and sisters not understanding him, and so on. The family I want to look at today just consisted of a brother and two sisters, but each shows us something that goes to make up the Christian family. (Reveal the words *The Christian Family* at the top of your board.)

A supper party was planned for Jesus, who of course brought along his disciples. Let us look at each member of the family. (As you refer to the various visual aids put them up.)

1. *Lazarus the witness* Refer to his recent death and his being raised to life by Jesus. He was a living witness to the power of Jesus, not so much by what he said but just because he was there. This should be true in the Christian home where parents know the power of Christ. Their lives should be a witness. It is what they are that counts just as much as what they say, though of course we must have a reason for the hope that is in us, and be prepared to say so when the occasion arises. Children are to be brought up 'in the fear and nurture of the Lord', as the old Marriage Service says.

2. *Martha the worker* We are told that Martha served (v. 2). I told as vividly as I could the other story of Martha and Mary in Luke 10: 38–42, ending with a free paraphrase of her words to Mary: 'You sit there doing nothing while I am working my fingers to the bone,' and Jesus' remarks to her, 'Martha, Martha, you are anxious and troubled about many things.'

Jesus was not rebuking her for doing the work but for being anxious about it. In a Christian family we should all be doing our work for the Lord. I once heard of a woman in London who actually had a notice over her sink, 'Divine Service performed here three times a day'. Adam had work to do before the Fall. The trouble with our fallen world today is not only that some cannot get work, but also that some do not want to work, and do not know how to use their spare time either. In a Christian home all should share in the work. The devil finds work for idle hands to do. In the Christian family children should learn to work heartily as to the Lord, and to know Paul's words, 'If a man won't work neither should he eat.'

3. *Mary the worshipper* I reminded the congregation about the sweet-smelling ointment that Mary poured over Jesus' feet. Mary was a worshipper. She was also the one who sat at Jesus' feet and listened to his teaching. I am sure that Jesus

would not have expected Martha to do all the work while Mary just sat at his feet. Hence in one version of the story in Luke 10 we are told that Mary '*also* sat at his feet'. Mary knew that whatever else had to be done one thing must not be omitted, and that was worship, costly worship. Refer to the price of the ointment.

What does our worship cost? (I put up the heart, and referred to grace and family prayers in the Christian home.)

It is quite extraordinary how other things get done when worship is put first. Is yours a Christian family where there is the witness of the home, the work of hands and the worship of hearts?

11. Palm Sunday: A Day of Contradictions

Aim

To show that central to the message of Palm Sunday is that Jesus is King and must become King of all aspects of our lives.

Texts

Zechariah 9:9 and Matthew 21:1–11.

Drama

50 Sketches for All Occasions 46 'The Dishonest Steward'.

Story

A long time ago the Second World War had just ended. But most young men at that time had to go through a period in the army (it was called National Service). For many young Christians it was a time when the challenge of being a Christian became very real.

It was the very first night in the barrack room for a certain young Christian recruit. What was he going to do about saying his normal end-of-the-day prayers? In those days it was quite usual for people to kneel by the side of their beds when they prayed. The young soldier thought to himself that perhaps he could just slip into his bunk and say his prayers under the blanket, but that would be a very poor witness to

Jesus, his Lord and Saviour. He must begin as he intended to go on. He quietly knelt at his bunk side. Jeers and cat-calls filled the air, followed by boots. He stayed on his knees till the other recruits got tired and fell asleep in their bunks. The following morning they woke to find all the boots that had been thrown, neatly lined up in the centre of the room – cleaned!

There was a hush in the barrack room the following evening when the young man knelt to say his prayers.

Hymns and songs

'Make way' (SOF 384); 'Prepare the way of the Lord' (SOF 473); 'Rejoice! Rejoice! Christ is in you' (SOF 480); 'Ride, ride on' (HTC 119); 'All glory, praise and honour' (HTC 120).

Prayers

400 Prayers 37, 263, 380, 381.

Main talk

Preparation

Prepare the following OHP acetates illustrating:

1. Jesus apparently about to throw himself from the pinnacle of the Temple.
2. A blank acetate with three acetate pictures attached:
   • Jesus on a donkey.
   • A crowd on left and right with space for Jesus.
   • Jesus on a horse.
3. Is Jesus King of our . . .
   • Moments? (Picture of clock.)
   • Mind? (Person with furrowed brow.)
   • Money? (A piggy-bank.)
   These should be able to be flipped over.

Presentation

Ask what a contradiction is. Explain that on the first Palm Sunday Jesus twice behaved in the opposite way to what might have been expected.

1. *Forcing choice* (OHP of Jesus on pinnacle of Temple.) At the beginning of his public ministry Jesus was tempted to throw himself down and be unharmed, so that everyone would follow him – but he refused.

During the ministry that followed he performed miracles of healing, but always told people to keep it quiet. He fed the five thousand, but then hid himself.

Now he comes out in public and fulfils the prophecy of Zechariah 9:9 (quote). (OHP of crowd with Jesus on donkey.) He declared himself King and everyone had to make up their minds.

We are constantly having to make decisions: which TV programme to watch, which clothes to buy, which food to eat, which crowd to follow, which party to vote for . . . We cannot sit on the fence for ever.

For three years people could make up their minds about Jesus, but now he forces them to do so, choosing a donkey of peace, not a horse of war; by cleansing the Temple; by very direct teaching. The religious leaders got the message and decided to have him killed.

Have you made up your mind about him? (Quote 2 Corinthians 6:2.)

Three devils were discussing how they could keep humans from following Jesus. One said, 'Tell them there's no heaven.' Another said, 'Tell them there's no hell.' But the one who got Satan's prize was the one who said, 'Tell them there's no hurry.'

2. *Peaceful strength* We usually admire the strong man. Our heroes are powerful. Give examples. The Jews thought that Jesus was going to help them be victorious over the Romans

who ruled Israel/Palestine. They thought he should come into Jerusalem on a horse. (OHP change donkey for horse.)

Zechariah spoke of war horses, but Jesus chose the gentle, peaceful donkey.

The world chooses armed force, the bomb and the bullet.

The great powers of Rome, France, Nazi Germany, etc. have chosen armed force and lost. The peaceful army of Jesus marches still. (Possibly quote from Romans 12:12–21; 2 Corinthians 10:3–4.)

Tell the story (above) of the new recruit and his prayers.

3. *Is Jesus our King?* (Show OHP.) Comment briefly on Christ's kingship of our moments, mind and money.

12. Who Crucified Jesus Christ?

Aim

To teach that Christ died for *our* sins, using a somewhat startling audio-visual aid.

Text

Acts 2:23.

Drama

50 Sketches for All Occasions 18 'Nailed!'.

Hymns and songs

'My Lord, what love is this' (SOF 398); 'There is a Redeemer' (SOF 544); 'How deep the Father's love for us' (SOF 780). The following hymns make specific reference to Jesus being nailed to the cross: 131, 133–135, 141 (HTC).

Prayers

400 Prayers 38, 39, 264–270.

Main talk

Preparation

With the aid of a fret-saw cut out the shape of a large hand in plywood and paint it pink. Prepare seven small thin cards with the following words printed in black on each side respectively:

Peter	Pride
Judas	Greed
Jews	Hate
Witnesses	Lying
Herod	Lust
Pilate	Selfishness

The last card should have *God* on one side and *Love* on the other in red. Have a hammer and seven large nails available.

Presentation

Begin the talk by asking the question, 'Who crucified Jesus Christ?' Agree that of course it was the soldiers, but that was only because it was their duty. Really they were the least to blame. There are two other answers.

First, you and I did. But you say, 'Not me! I would never have done that.' That is what Peter said. But Peter crucified Jesus by his pride. (Produce the card with *Peter* on one side and *Pride* on the other.) Peter boasted he would never deny Jesus and then denied him only a few hours later. Have you ever been proud? You and I crucify Jesus Christ by pride (nail *Pride* to the hand).

In the same way enlarge on *Judas, Jews, Witnesses, Herod* and *Pilate*. (Nail these to the hand also.) You and I crucified Jesus Christ. What are we doing about it? There is nothing we can do about it.

Someone else crucified Jesus Christ: God! God sent his Son into the world to die for us. Jesus said, 'No man takes my life from me.' Later he said, 'Not my will but yours be done.' To Pilate he said, 'You would have no power over me unless it had been given you from above.' God sent Jesus to the cross because he loves us. (Show the card with *God* on one side and *Love* on the other and nail it to the other side of the hand.)

So Jesus died because of our sins and for our sins. If you find this message astonishing then listen to the words of Peter in his first sermon on the day of Pentecost. Quote Acts 2:23 slowly. End by exhorting the congregation to receive Jesus as Saviour.

13. Pay Day (Good Friday)

Aim

To explain the meaning of the cross; especially topical if used on Good Friday.

Text

Romans 6:23.

Drama

50 Sketches for All Occasions 24 'Home Improvements'.

Hymns and songs

'Come and see' (SOF 67); 'You laid aside Your majesty' (SOF 633); 'At the foot of the cross' (SOF 662); 'There is a green hill far away' (HTC 148).

Prayers

400 Prayers 30, 39, 264–270.

Main talk

Preparation

Either simply have a twenty pound note available or, if you or a member of your congregation have the necessary ability, paint a large note on a piece of cardboard with a piece of card that can be pulled out from one side, with the words 'Wages for Work' on it. On the back of the twenty pound note have a skull and crossbones and the words 'I promise to pay death', and pull out 'Wages of Sin'.

Presentation

Begin by talking about pay day. Show twenty pound note and 'Wages for Work'. Talk about the twenty pound note as being a promise from the chief cashier of the Bank of England to pay twenty pounds sterling, and comment on the Sovereign's head appearing on the note as a guarantee of its trustworthiness.

But work is not the only thing for which we deserve a wage. Turn over the visual aid if you are using the larger one and show that God promises that the wages for sin is death.

Illustrate this from the stories of Adam and Eve, Achan, King Saul, Judas, etc. But we don't have to look just to the Bible for illustrations. We know it in practical experience – the misuse of money, sex and drugs teaches us this. Go on to say, however, that this Friday is *pay day* in another sense. On Good Friday Jesus, the sinless Son of God, deliberately allowed sinful men to nail him to a cross, and while he hung from it God his Father turned his face from him and allowed him to suffer hell – that is spiritual death – for us. Jesus died the death you and I deserve. He paid the wages of sin once and for all.

> There was no other good enough
> To pay the price of sin:
> He only could unlock the gate
> Of heaven and let us in.

Now all those who repent of their sins and believe in Jesus Christ as their Saviour are promised the free gift of eternal life from God – and God never breaks a promise.

Does Friday mean pay day for you?

14. Why Did God Allow the Cross?

Aim

To explain why Jesus had to die and to attempt to give a reason why God does not intervene to prevent disasters. The talk could be used on Good Friday.

Text

Matthew 27:46.

Drama

50 Sketches for All Occasions 7 'The Passion'; or 8 'Nailed!'.

Hymns and songs

Good Friday section of hymn book; 'For this purpose' (SOF 114); 'The price is paid' (SOF 540); 'I believe there is a God in heaven' (SOF 788).

Prayers

400 Prayers 38, 39, 264–270, 364, 365.

Main talk

Preparation

Obtain a marionette, ie a puppet worked by strings.

Presentation

Begin by discussing with your congregation the problem of the terrible disasters that happen in the world, perhaps mentioning a recent one.

Introduce your marionette. Show how it jumps entirely to your tune, as you pull its strings. Ask if it can love anyone. Hence explain how men and women have had to be given some real degree of free will, which means they can choose how they will behave. If they had not, then they would be no different from puppets on strings. Part of the story in Genesis 2–3 could be mentioned.

Now if God always intervened every time we did something bad or stupid we would simply become puppets. Sometimes people are very irresponsible. Men who run coal mines are told that a coal tip is slipping and could engulf a school full of children. If they do nothing and it happens, as it did years ago in a Welsh mining village, who is to blame: God or the owners of the mine?

However, we know God cares, because Jesus, his Son, came into the world, lived a perfect life, but eventually was taken prisoner, condemned to death because he claimed to be God (which was true), and was nailed to a cross to die. From that cross Jesus cried, 'My God, my God, why have you forsaken me?' God did not intervene even then, even though it was his own Son dying there in terrible agony. Why? For the same reason that he has given men freedom to behave in such a terrible way if they so choose. But also, in this case, because Jesus was dying for the sins of the world. That is how much God cares. Let us always remember this when the next disaster happens.

15. No Separation from God's Love

Aim

To acknowledge that we all need love and that perfect love is found in God alone.

Text

Romans 8:31–39.

Drama

50 Sketches for All Occasions 33 'Love is . . .'; 34 'God's love is like . . .'; 44 'The Prodigal Daughter'.

Hymns and songs

'Great is the Lord' (SOF 145); 'I could sing unending songs' (SOF 790); 'No eye has seen' (SOF 943).

Prayers

400 Prayers 60, 196, 240, 400, 401.

Main talk

Preparation

On an OHP acetate draw a wall. The central part of the wall should be a separate piece of acetate shaped like a cross (shown by the outlined area in fig. 1) and laid over the wall so that it is not evident at the start.

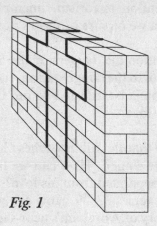

Fig. 1

On a large heart-shaped piece of acetate print the word GOD. On four circles a little smaller than the heart, illustrate 'trials' (eg a sad face), 'the future' (eg a bomb exploding), 'evil powers' (eg a devil) and 'death' (eg a tombstone). These can be flipped into place as you refer to them.

Presentation

If it is likely to be known, refer to the Beatles' song 'All you need is love' and proceed to point out the universal need for love, with reference to children's need for parental love. Then state that most of all we need the love of God. Refer to the OHP, revealing the wall already in place. Put the word GOD on the far side of the wall.

We often feel that there are big barriers between us and God's love. (As you refer to the different things, put up the words on the near side of the wall.)

1. *Trials* Paul faced many (v. 35). Enlarge briefly on the sort of trials that the congregation might have. Mention that some of these come because we stand up for Jesus, but we can feel very alone and God's love can seem far away.

2. *The future* Mention terrorism, unemployment, illness, loneliness, etc. Can we be sure of God's provision and love?

3. *Evil powers* Mention the dangers of the occult, with illustrations appropriate to the congregation, such as fascination with horoscopes, ouija boards and so on. Could we be separated from God's love?

4. *Death* We know that the Bible teaches God is love, but he is also holy. We are sinners. How can we face God beyond death? Will we be separated from his love?

Finally, refer to verses 37–39. How can we be so certain? Perhaps tell the story of Abraham's near-sacrifice of his son, Isaac.

Now remove the piece of acetate on the front of the wall to reveal a cross-shaped way through the wall (fig. 2). God did not spare his only Son. If we have repented and believed, then we have nothing to fear. Whatever we feel, God's love is near. Mention Jesus' death, resurrection, ascension and intercession at the Father's side. Finish by quoting verse 34, possibly also Romans 5:1–2.

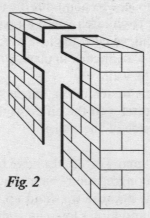

Fig. 2

16. Easter Eggs

Aim

To retell the Easter story and make a single point – that Jesus is our Master – using simple visual aids held by children.

Text

John 20:16 (AV).

Drama

Scenes and Wonders 'Easter Eggs and Easter Errors', p. 28.

Hymns and songs

See Easter section in church hymn book; 'Come on and celebrate' (SOF 73); 'Jesus, we celebrate Your victory' (SOF 309); 'Led like a lamb' (SOF 322).

Prayers

400 Prayers 41, 42, 271, 385.

Main talk

Preparation

Cut out six cards in different colours in the shape of large eggs, with E on one card, A on the next and so on, to spell the word 'EASTER'. On the back of the first 'E', print an 'M' in the same size as the other letters.

Presentation

Ask the children who had Easter eggs today. Ask for five volunteers to hold cards. Then draw out from the children the Easter story. Who first came to find Jesus? What time of the day was it? Draw out from the children the word 'early' and produce the first 'E', which you hold up yourself.

Where was Jesus' body buried? Draw out the word 'tomb', produce the 'T' of Easter and hand it to a child to hold up.

Who did the tomb belong to? Draw out the words 'Joseph of Arimathaea' and produce the 'A', which you hand to another child to hold up.

What was in front of the tomb? Draw out the words 'stone', 'soldiers' and 'seal', and put the 'S' in front of 'T'. What did the women find when they got to the tomb? Draw out the word 'empty' and perhaps make reference to the 'earthquake' and put the next 'E' up. What was the message of the angel? That Jesus was risen. Produce the 'R'.

Talk about Mary of Magdala, who remained in the garden weeping. Mention how the Lord Jesus had said her many sins were forgiven. Jesus had brought her a new life, but now she thought he was dead and everything was over. Suddenly she saw the gardener and asked him where Jesus had been laid. Then she discovered that the gardener was after all Jesus. Ask the children what Mary called him. Assuming you have had read the Authorised version of the story you should be able to draw out the answer 'Master' and turn round the first 'E' of EASTER to reveal the 'M' – so spelling 'MASTER'.

Ask the congregation whether Jesus is their Master too.

17. The Broken Easter Egg

Aim

To convey the evidence for the resurrection of Jesus using the illustration of a broken Easter egg.

Text

Acts 1:3.

Drama

50 Sketches for All Occasions 10 'Jesus is Back'; 11 'Sherlock Holmes Investigates . . . The Case of the Missing Corpse'; *Acting Up* pp. 93–4 'Easter Morning'.

Hymns and songs

Easter section of church hymn book, especially HTC 162 'These are the facts as we have received them'; 'All heaven declares' (SOF 10); 'I believe in Jesus' (SOF 203); 'He has risen' (SOF 753).

Prayers

400 Prayers 41, 42, 271, 385.

Main talk

Preparation

Construct out of cardboard a large flat Easter egg, say about 3′ 4″ maximum length and 2′ 3″ maximum width. Divide the egg up into five pieces as illustrated, the centre piece having the words, preferably in yellow fluorescent paper, 'Jesus Risen' on it. The other four pieces, which could be covered with different coloured fluorescent paper, should have the words, and possibly illustrations of, 'Empty Tomb', 'Bible', 'The Church', and 'Changed Disciples'. Three other pieces of white card similar in shape to the piece in the centre of the egg, but not identical, should have the words on them 'Fable', 'Fancy' and 'Body Stolen'. Either fix the pieces onto a Teazlegraph board or fix some drawing pins in discreet places to hold each piece in place. The visuals could also be done on an OHP.

Presentation

Explain that there are various reasons for believing the Easter story. Why should we doubt the biblical account, remembering that the writers got no royalties for their work and in some cases suffered and died for their testimony to Jesus? No one who has studied the evidence with an open mind can deny that the tomb was empty. Comment on the condition of the grave-clothes, the remarkable change in the frightened disciples, and the coming into existence of the Christian church. As you talk about each of these things, place the different parts of the egg onto a board so that the egg is gradually formed in front of the congregation's eyes, but with the centre piece missing.

How do we account for these facts? One suggestion is that the disciples stole the body. Refer to Matthew 28:11–15, and say how impossible the idea really is. Attempt to fit the piece 'Body Stolen' into the egg and ask whether it fits.

Next discuss the idea of 'Fancy', explaining how the disciples may have imagined that they saw Jesus. Point out that in fact they were not expecting to see him and on a number of occasions mistook him for someone else first (eg Mary Magdalene in the garden, two disciples on the Emmaus Road), which is not the way hallucinations work. Attempt to fit 'Fancy' into the egg, but unsuccessfully.

Next try 'Fable', explaining how someone has suggested that the Christian story evolved rather mysteriously like many fables associated with other religions. Point out that there is plenty of evidence in Israel today for the existence of Jesus as well as plenty of historical evidence. 'This was not done in a corner,' the apostle Paul told King Agrippa. Attempt to fit in 'Fable', also unsuccessfully.

Finally, pick up the shape 'Jesus Risen' and discover that it fits. Briefly recap how this is the one explanation of the various items round the egg and ask whether the congregation know the risen Jesus for themselves.

18. God's Easter Egg

Aim

To show the meaning of Easter using a large Easter egg and various objects that can be pulled out of it.

Text

1 Corinthians 15:1–4, 55–56.

Drama

Scenes and Wonders 'Easter Eggs and Easter Errors', p. 28.

Hymns and songs

See Easter section of church hymn book; 'Thank you, Jesus' (SOF 523); 'I will offer up my life' (SOF 851); 'Thank you for saving me' (SOF 1015).

Prayers

400 Prayers 41, 42, 271, 385.

Main talk

Preparation

Draw on cardboard a large egg (about 3' 4" maximum height and 2' 3" maximum width). Paint the egg with attractive colours and put ribbon round the middle. Cut three rectangular strips of cardboard out of the egg and write the following words on paper to stick behind the gaps: 'Death defeated', 'Sinners saved', 'Life loosed'. Replace the rectangular pieces of card that you cut out from your egg and attach to the egg by means of nylon thread. (See Talk 4.) Into the egg also slot the following flannelgraph or Teazlegraph visual aids that can be pulled out: a small chicken, a handkerchief with a blot on it and one without a blot on it, a skull and a cross.

Presentation

Ask children at the service whether they had an Easter egg for Easter. Ask whether any of them had Easter eggs with something inside them. Explain that today we are going to think about God's Easter egg and reveal the egg. What do we find in it?

1. *Death defeated* Reveal these words. Pull out the skull and place across it the cross. Explain how Christ's death and resurrection defeated death. Our weekly Christian worship on Sundays is a reminder that Christ rose from the dead on the

first day of the week victorious over death. Yet despite this weekly reminder most people (including many Christians) do not know that death is defeated (refer to 2 Timothy 1:10 and the Easter Proper Preface in the *Book of Common Prayer* and *Common Worship*).

2. *Sinners saved* Pull out handkerchief with blot on it. This is a picture of any life. All of us are sinners, but Jesus died to take away sin. How do we know that sinners can be saved? The resurrection is the proof that Jesus died for our sins. Refer to 1 John 1:7 and Isaiah 44:22–23. Pull out the other handkerchief that is clean.

3. *Life loosed* Produce chicken and refer to new life and how, when Jesus rose from the dead and came out of the tomb, life was loosed. He would never die again and those who trust him as their Saviour can receive new life and need not fear physical death, for he has conquered it.

19. Easter, Seed Time and Baptism

Aim

To use the season of spring and seed time to illustrate truths relating to Easter and the Christian life, including baptism.

Text

John 12:24–25.

Drama

If there is a baptism in the service, that is dramatic in itself.

Hymns and songs

'I am a new creation' (SOF 197); 'Rejoice!' (SOF 480); 'Who is there like you?' (SOF 1117).

Prayers

400 Prayers 41, 42, 56, 271, 385.

Main talk

Preparation

Either have three large cards (say, 30″ high by 20″ wide) that can be placed completely onto a Teazlegraph board side by side, or make three acetates for an OHP. Onto each card/acetate put the following:

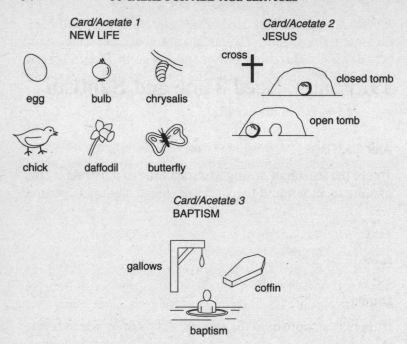

Card/Acetate 1
NEW LIFE

egg   bulb   chrysalis

chick   daffodil   butterfly

Card/Acetate 2
JESUS

cross   closed tomb

open tomb

Card/Acetate 3
BAPTISM

gallows   coffin

baptism

Have a small table lamp available connected to an electric socket.

Presentation

Pick up the table lamp and switch it on. Then remove the bulb and ask if anyone will come up and put their fingers across the terminals inside the socket for a small prize. 'But surely if you are a Christian you will not be hurt.' Agree with the congregation that that will make no difference and that God works according to certain fixed laws. If we are so stupid as to touch electric terminals we will get a nasty shock. From there talk about another law of nature that we see all around us at this time of year.

1. *New life* Put up first card or acetate. Bulbs that had been planted in the ground a while ago are now producing beautiful daffodils. But other things seem to go through a sort of death before coming to new life, like eggs and chicks, and chrysalises and butterflies. This is another law of nature: the way God works in his world.

2. *Jesus* In the text Jesus is saying that like a grain of wheat he will have to go through a sort of death before coming to new life again. Put up second card or acetate and enlarge on the Easter story. The same law is true for Christians.

3. *Baptism* Explain how we have to go through a kind of death to our old life if we are going to be raised to new life. This is symbolised by baptism (see Romans 6:3–7). Put up third card or acetate. But the same law is true for our everyday Christian life (v.25). Like John the Baptist we know that Jesus must increase in our lives and we must decrease (John 3:30). Finally at the end of our lives we have to go through death before we enter into the new life of heaven that God has prepared for us. Perhaps refer to the teaching of 1 Corinthians 15:35–36, 42–44 and the resurrection body God has prepared for those who believe.

Conclude with the story of the American evangelist, D. L. Moody, who used to say that one day people would report that D. L. Moody was dead. 'Don't believe them! I shall be more alive than anyone on earth.'

20. Ascension Promises

Aim

To show that two very important promises were made at the time of the Ascension concerning the coming of the Holy Spirit and the return of Jesus.

It is assumed that this talk will be given on Ascension Day itself or the Sunday following. It might be quite easily adapted to be given during the Advent season.

Texts

Acts 1:1–11; see also John 14:3, 16–17.

Drama

50 Sketches for All Occasions 13 'A Farewell Present'. It is quite effective if the three disciples walk slowly up the church conversing, but it is essential that either they have loud voices or are all wearing microphones.

Hymns and songs

'Breathe on me' (SOF 677); 'Father of creation' (SOF 714); 'Give me, Lord, a dream from heaven' (SOF 727).

Prayers

400 Prayers 47–50, 215, 256, 272, 393.

Main talk

Preparation

Obtain or draw (possibly for use on an OHP) a picture of a space rocket. Make two large rail tickets with the words *Earth to Heaven* on one and *Heaven to Earth* on the other. 'Clip' the first one. Make eleven large cards that can be held up by children so that all the congregation can see the numbers written on them. Two of the cards will need to be larger than the others. On ten of the cards have the numbers one to ten. On the back of the first card either have the words *Holy Spirit* or have a picture depicting the Spirit such as a flame or a dove. On the eleventh card have a large question mark, and on the back *Coming soon Jesus*. Have the means of making a loud noise! Have a mock-up newspaper with headline *JESUS CHRIST RETURNED YESTERDAY*.

Presentation

Showing the rocket, talk about launching it by countdown. Involving ten children call out the numbers from ten to one and get each child to raise their number above their head. Immediately after one is raised sound the loud noise.

Explain that at the time of the Ascension, when Jesus returned to his Father in heaven, two countdowns began, both of which looked forward to events that were promised would happen sooner or later.

1. *The countdown to Pentecost* (*the coming of the Holy Spirit*)
Repeat the countdown using the cards, but when reaching the last card ask the child holding it to turn it round, revealing *Holy Spirit* (or illustration). Explain how Jesus promised that the Spirit would be sent shortly after Jesus returned to heaven (see Acts 1:4–5, 8; John 14:16–17). He actually came *ten* days after Jesus left, on the day we call Whitsunday or Pentecost.

2. *The countdown to the Parousia* (*the second coming of Jesus*)
Now we have a big problem, because though there is a day
when Jesus will return we cannot do the countdown because
Jesus has not told us when it is. Get a child to hold up the
eleventh card with the question mark, then to turn it round
to reveal *Coming soon Jesus*. Perhaps quote from Acts 1:6–7
and Matthew 24:36.

3. *Why do Christians believe Jesus is coming back?* Show the
giant rail tickets and explain that the first half has been used
(hence the 'clip'), but the return half has not yet been used.
We know it will be, even though we do not know when,
because he promised (John 14:3) and so did the angels (Acts
1:10–11). In his life on earth Jesus told his disciples that he
would be crucified (he was); that he would rise from the dead
and ascend to his Father (he did); that he would send the
Holy Spirit (he came); that there would be a church (there
is). Jesus keeps his promises. Just because he has not
returned yet does not mean that he will not.

4. *What will happen when Jesus returns?* Such an event is
surely to be newsworthy. Do you think we might see head-
lines like this: *JESUS CHRIST RETURNED YESTER-
DAY*? Draw out the point that when Jesus comes it will be
the end of the world, so there will be no more newspapers,
but Christians will go to be with the Lord to be rewarded
according to how they used their lives. Others will be judged
for their sins.

5. *What difference does Jesus' promise to return make now?*
Compare the difference of looking forward to a friend who
is (say) returning from abroad and a rent collector. (See
Matthew 24:45–25:13; 2 Peter 3:10–14.)

Note

This talk was based on an idea provided by the Revd Andrew
Hetherington, at the time an incumbent in Bootle,
Merseyside, and now Team Rector, West Swindon.

21. Pentecost: Wind, Tongues and Fire

Aim

To give a simple explanation of the coming of the Holy Spirit to the church on the Day of Pentecost.

Text

Acts 2:1–4 (or possibly to v. 21).

Story/Drama

See story in talk below. *50 Sketches for All Occasions* 13 'A Farewell Present'; 14 'Language Barrier'. See note in Talk 20.

Hymns and songs

'Spirit of the living God' (SOF 510); 'He is the Lord' (SOF 755); 'Is anyone thirsty?' (SOF 823).

Prayers

400 Prayers 51, 52, 200, 235, 371, 395.

Main talk

Preparation

Have a recording on a cassette player of a foreign language being spoken. You will also need a whistle and a pair of fire bellows.

Presentation

Assuming the talk is being given on Whitsunday (Pentecost), ask what day it is. What do we often receive on special days, like Christmas or birthdays? On obtaining the answer of presents or gifts, ask what gift the disciples received that day. What do we mean by the Holy Spirit? Let us see what we can learn from the reading we heard this morning (assuming that the text above and further verses were read).

1. *Tongues* Play the recording of the foreign language. Ask if anyone can understand it. Possibly someone might; others may know the language, even if they cannot translate. Read verse 4 of text. Clearly a miracle was taking place. The disciples could probably only speak Aramaic and Greek, yet the crowds gathered in Jerusalem for the festival were hearing them speak in a wide variety of languages, depending on where they were born. Ask whether we should refer to the Holy Spirit as 'he' or 'it'. Draw out that he must be a person, because things don't speak. If challenged, point out that cassette players and radios are reproducing people's voices. Explain that the Holy Spirit is the third person of the Holy Trinity that we refer to when saying the Creed and the Grace (2 Corinthians 13:14). It was very important that he helped the disciples to speak, because they, and we today, are to use the gift of speech to worship God (Acts 2:11) and to witness to the Lord Jesus (Acts 1:8).

2. *Sound* Blow the whistle. What are you hearing? Explain that they were hearing the sound of wind, and it was the sound of wind that those first disciples heard. Explain that that was very appropriate for the coming of the Spirit, because the Spirit is very like a wind. Indeed in Greek the words for wind, breath and spirit are all the same word – *pneuma* – from which we get words like 'pneumatic', which

we use to describe a drill that works by compressed air, or a tyre filled with air. Neither the wind nor the Spirit can be seen, but we often know they are there by the sound. Peter preached to the crowds, but it was more than Peter speaking, for they also heard the inner voice of the Holy Spirit speaking, leading them to repent and believe.

3. *Fire* Produce fire bellows and ask what they are. Explain that in places where it is legal to have open fires they can help a fire to burn more brightly. Obviously the tongues of fire that fell on the disciples were unique, but it was a very appropriate sign because John the Baptist had said earlier that Jesus would baptise with the Holy Spirit and with fire (Luke 3:16). That is what the disciples were experiencing. It changed their lives and led them to preach boldly about the need to turn from sin, to trust in the Lord Jesus Christ for salvation, to receive the Holy Spirit and to lead holy lives.

A boy I used to teach at a boarding preparatory school suddenly changed for the better, and began reading his Bible and praying before he went to bed. On enquiry it turned out that the change came after a church service the entire school had attended. Others had heard the same sermon, but it had not had any particular effect. This boy had heard not just the preacher, but the voice of God the Holy Spirit, and we all knew because we saw the change in his life. (Either adapt this story or use a similar one from your own experience.)

Might the same Holy Spirit be speaking in that way to some here this morning? Then you should respond by repenting of your sins, trusting in Jesus for salvation and receive the special gift of the Holy Spirit that those disciples received on the first Whitsunday.

22. What's New?

Aim

To explain what was new for humanity when the Holy Spirit was poured out at Pentecost.

Texts

(a) Joel 2:28–29; (b) Jeremiah 31:31–34; (c) Ezekiel 36:26–27; (d) Isaiah 12:1–2.

Drama

50 Sketches for All Occasions 13 'A Farewell Present'.

Hymns and songs

'Peace like a river' (SOF 459); 'Give me, Lord, a dream of heaven' (SOF 727); 'My lips shall praise You' (SOF 937).

Prayers

400 Prayers 51, 52, 200, 235, 371, 395.

Main talk

Preparation
Arrange for different members of the congregation to read the four passages listed above.

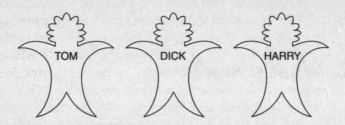

Have on two pieces of card covered with Teazlegraph material the letters *Tri* and *Unity*. Cut out from different coloured day-glo card three figures and print across their middles *Tom*, *Dick* and *Harry*. Make from card two 'tables' to represent the stone tables for the Ten Commandments. Cut out of day-glo card (in pink or red) a heart shape, some enlarged musical notes (or people obviously praising), on white card a picture of an open Bible, on pink card a picture of praying hands, on any colour card a picture of a gift (decorative string can be put round it) and on yellow card cut out eight shapes that look like tongues of fire, sticking one on the centre of the heart. On all these visuals stick Velcro, ready for use on the Teazlegraph board, or OHP.

Presentation

Refer to the Creed said in the service. Who did we say we believed in? Draw out the word 'Trinity' and using the cards with *Tri* and *Unity* show how the word was derived. Explain that in a sense we are each trinities of body, mind and spirit.

Ask if the congregation think God has always existed. And Jesus the Son? And what about the Holy Spirit? Draw out that though the Holy Spirit has always existed, we do not hear much about him in the Old Testament.

Ask what is special about Whitsunday and what happened on the first Whitsunday. The Holy Spirit has always been around, yet on the first Whitsunday he was sent to the church. What was new about his coming?

1. *He comes to anyone* Normally one had to be a very special person in Old Testament days to have God's Spirit: prophet, king, specially wise or very artistic. He was promised to the nation generally, but not to individuals particularly. Moses longed that all God's people might be prophets. But Joel made a wonderful prophecy (quote a). So the Spirit is now for all, ie for Tom, Dick and Harry. He's for everyone in this church today, just for the asking. If we repent of sin and ask Jesus to be Saviour, we are promised the gift of the Spirit. (Place 'tongues of fire' over the heads of the three figures of Tom, Dick and Harry on the Teazlegraph board.)

2. *He comes into our lives* In the Old Testament days God gave his people the Ten Commandments (put up tables of stone on board). If they obeyed all would be well. The trouble was that they did not obey because they had no power within themselves to do so (quotes b and c). (Put up the heart with the 'tongues' in the centre of it.) The quotations spoke of God coming to live within us by his Spirit. Refer to William Temple's famous observation that he could not compose music like Beethoven or paint pictures like Turner without the spirit of those artists coming to live within him. Nor could he live a life like Jesus without the Spirit of Jesus coming within him. But that is exactly what God promised him could happen.

3. *He comes in fullness* No one in former days knew anything like the experience of the Spirit that the early church came to know. Isaiah had some vision of it (quote d). Use the remaining visual aids with 'tongues' over each to illustrate:

- A new sense of worship and praise
- A new ability to understand the Scriptures
- A new depth in prayer
- New gifts for all: tongues, prophecy, healing, wisdom, discernment, ministry.

Does everyone here know the infilling of the Spirit?

23. Revival

Aim

To teach how the church can be revived and to stress the need for a balance between emphasis on the word of God and emphasis on the Spirit. Suitable for Whitsunday.

Text

Ezekiel 37:1–14.

Drama

50 Sketches for All Occasions 14 'Language Barrier'.

Hymns and songs

'Shine, Jesus, shine' (SOF 362); 'Spirit of the living God' (SOF 511); 'These are the days of Elijah' (SOF 1047); 'We want to see Jesus lifted high' (SOF 1105).

Prayers

400 Prayers 51, 52, 59, 200, 235, 249, 371, 395.

Main talk

Preparation

Prepare for the Teazlegraph board the words *How is the*

church to be revived? Hear the WORD of God, and *Receive the WIND of God*. WORD could be written on the background of an open Bible and WIND could have a letter each on four simple kites cut out of different colours of day-glo paper, with short lengths of string trailing from them. (This was particularly appropriate when this talk was given its first airing, because the family service was followed by a church picnic at which there was a kite-flying competition.) Also cut out of white paper lots of bones and skulls.

Presentation

Refer to people being taken into slavery, illustrating with modern examples such as the Jews in Nazi Germany. Then refer back to about 600 BC when Ezekiel was prophesying. He had a vision, a kind of dream with a definite message. He saw a valley, or plain, with many skeletons on the ground. The bones were very dry, implying that they had been there a long time. Ask what that might mean and draw out that they represented Israel and Judah, who had been depressed and hopeless for ten years. (Put up bones and skulls at bottom of board.)

Ezekiel heard a voice – 'Ezekiel, can these bones live?' Ask whose voice. Ezekiel thought that the obvious answer was 'no', so why ask? Perhaps God had a message of hope. He replied, 'O Lord God, you know.'

1. *Hear the WORD of God* Tell the story in verses 4–8 and put up the words on the board about a quarter of the way down. Ask if the army lived. What was still needed?

2. *Receive the WIND of God* Continue the story in verses 9–10 and explain about the need for breath. Perhaps refer to Adam being created by God, but still needing breath to bring him to life. Refer to the four winds which meant the four corners of the earth. Explain that the words *breath*,

wind and *spirit* are all the same word in Hebrew. In Greek *wind* and *spirit* are the same word (*pneuma*) from which we get words like *pneumatic*. The army had to receive the *WIND of God* (put up words on the board). This was a message to the whole nation. One day there would be revival and the united nation. One day there would be revival and the united nation would return to its own country.

What does it have to say to us in the church? Many churches in our land seem lifeless and hopeless, which is why so many are increasingly empty. It has been said that if the Holy Spirit left the church 90 per cent of what the church does would continue to happen without anyone noticing!

Perhaps tell the story of a cemetery that had to restrict the number being buried in it to the local parish only. A notice was erected: '*This cemetery is for the dead living in this parish*'! Comment that there are many dead living in our parishes – 'dead in trespasses and sins' – and perhaps there are some here.

3. *How is the church to be revived?* (Put up these words at top of the board.) Refer to the two statements below this question and comment along these lines: *WORD of God* – the need for biblical preaching, home Bible study groups and private Bible reading to discover what God's word means to us today. *WIND of God* – it is not enough to know God's word, we have to be living it. The original disciples knew Jesus' word to them, but they did not live it till after receiving the Spirit at Pentecost.

We have to be open to the Spirit of God as a church, that we may receive all his gifts and show forth his fruit of love, joy, peace . . . then we shall know revivial. It could begin today.

24. Harvest: Weeds and Wheat

Aim

To help people see the need to accept Christ as Saviour before it is too late.

Text

Matthew 13:24–30, 36–43.

Drama

50 Sketches for All Occasions 15 'The Jam Factory'. *Acting Up* 'In the Beginning' Parts I and II pp. 7–10. Note that there is quite a lot of action in the talk itself.

Hymns and songs

Select from Harvest section in church hymn book. 'Here I am' (SOF 167); 'Oh, heaven is in my heart' (SOF 416); 'He made the earth' (SOF 756).

Prayers

400 Prayers 94, 107, 119, 274.

Main talk

Preparation

1. *Wheat and tares* Dr Plumptre, writing in Ellicott's *Bible Commentary for English Readers*, relates that the act of an enemy sowing tares among wheat

> was then – and still is – a common form of Eastern malice or revenge. It easily escaped detection. It inflicted both loss and trouble. The 'enemy' had the satisfaction of brooding for weeks or months over the prospect of the injury he had inflicted, and the vexation it would cause when discovered. The tares, known to botanists as the *Lolium temulentum*, or *darnel*, grew up at first with stalk and blade like the wheat; it was not till fructification began that the difference was easily detected. It adds to the point of the parable to remember that the seeds of the tares were not merely useless as food, but were positively noxious.

This is really the main point of the parable, namely that just as wheat and tares initially look very much alike, so to begin with can those who have accepted Jesus Christ as their Saviour and those who have not. Therefore, we who profess and call ourselves Christians must not be too quick to judge one another – that is solely God's prerogative. Our primary task as teachers of the word of God is to lead people to a saving knowledge of Christ or, in the language of the farmer, to sow seeds in people's hearts that will bring forth fruit to eternal life. We ourselves shall frequently not be at all sure, perhaps for some time, which people have really responded to God's word, but fortunately we are not judged by our success but by our faithfulness in teaching what he has told us. The parable under consideration here brings especial need for honesty and faithfulness, for it undoubtedly teaches the fact of both heaven and hell.

2. *God's love and justice* The twin doctrines of God's love for sinners and his judgement on sin must not be separated. The Bible clearly teaches both. For us to accept one and reject the other means that we really deny the Bible as our ultimate authority, and, if we do that, we cannot really be sure even of God's love. In fact, there is no antagonism between his love and his justice. They both met at Calvary, where we see demonstrated God's love for us sinners and his judgement on our sins. In this lesson, therefore, we must make clear that those who persist in sin and refuse God's loving offer of salvation will one day be judged and, like the tares, destroyed. The point to stress, however, is that if this should happen it is our fault – not God's. Hell was never prepared for man but for the devil and his angels (cf Matthew 25:34, 41).

'Those who are tares today may be wheat tomorrow' (St Augustine).

3. *Visual aid* Prepare seven pieces of cardboard folded in the middle horizontally, with the following words:

on the top half:
Farmer Field Wheat Enemy Tares Harvest Barn
on the bottom half:
Jesus World Saved Devil Lost End-of-World   Heaven

It is helpful if the words 'Farmer', 'Wheat' and 'Barn' are printed on a yellow background, 'Enemy' and 'Tares' on a red background, 'Field' on green and 'Harvest' on orange. The actual lettering for 'Farmer', 'Wheat' and 'Barn' could be printed in green and the lettering of 'Jesus', 'Saved' and 'Heaven' printed in red. All other lettering should be black.

The fold in the cards should be made by cutting the front with a sharp, single-edged razor blade, the pressure being insufficient to cut right through the card. It is wise also to put a strip of Sellotape along the back of the fold.

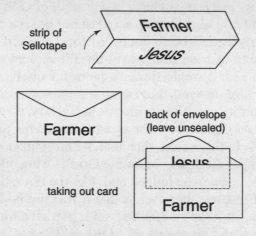

These envelopes could be gummed or pinned on a board if you have too few children to hold them.

4. *Before the service* Before the harvest service, select seven children whom you can rely on, say five boys and two girls, and distribute the cards among them, the girls holding 'Field' and 'Harvest'. Tell them to come up to the front immediately before your talk and sit on seven chairs you have placed in front for the purpose. Tell the children that when they hear you mention in your talk the word on the top of their card they should stand up and show the top of their card to everyone else, keeping the lower half bent back so that it is out of view. During the second part of your talk the children should bend the lower part of their card down, when the word on it has been guessed by the other children listening. Mention also to the children holding 'Field', 'Enemy', 'Tares' and 'Harvest' to be ready to sit down just before your talk ends, when you indicate.

Presentation

Jesus often liked to tell stories to the people. He would perhaps be sitting in a boat by the seaside with the people on the beach. One day he caught sight of a sower sowing his seed on a hillside (point to an imaginary sower in the distance), and so he used this as the subject for a story. Of course, Jesus was rather like a sower himself, sowing seeds of ideas into people's minds and hearts. That will also happen today, as I tell you one of his stories. Let us pray that the seeds that fall into our minds and hearts now may grow and bring forth fruit to eternal life. (Short prayer.)

1. *Wheat and tares* Tell as vividly as you can the parable of the tares among the wheat, emphasising that wheat and tares look alike in the early days of growth. Your retelling of the parable will be more effective if you have read the story many times over yourself beforehand and then retold it to yourself aloud without notes. Added effect can be given (say) by rubbing your hands together as you imagine the enemy gloating over what he has done as he thinks about the tares growing up without the farmer knowing. As you tell the story, be sure to mention in order the seven words on the top of your cards and glance towards the children helping you to ensure that each stands up at the right moment.

2. *Disciples question Jesus* Having told the story, mention how Jesus told other stories and then sent the people away. The disciples of Jesus, however, later gathered round him and asked him to explain the parable, which he did. Now throw the interpretation of the parable to the children by asking them to explain it for you.

'Who do you think the farmer was?' (Mention that you have already given them a hint, for before your prayer you should have said that Jesus was like a sower.) Having received the answer that the farmer is Jesus, see that the child holding the card bends down the lower part to reveal the word 'Jesus' on it. Proceed now to draw from the other children that the field is the world and get the lower part of that card displayed.

Consider now who Jesus' enemy is (ie do not deal with wheat yet). Discuss briefly the great battle that is going on in the world between Jesus and the devil. Something of this battle was seen in Bible days, for example when Herod killed all the baby boys in Bethlehem at the first Christmas time; the temptation in the wilderness at the beginning of Jesus' ministry; and the temptation to escape the cross in the Garden of Gethsemane. Jesus was completely triumphant, but still the war rages, even though the devil knows he is a defeated enemy. This battle rages in the hearts of boys and girls, men and women.

Those who follow Jesus are called in the parable – what? (Wheat.) Turn down the word 'Saved'. Those who follow the devil are called what? (Tares.) Turn down the word 'Lost'. Explain that just as we saw that wheat and tares are difficult to tell apart at first, so are the saved and lost. Each of us knows whether we have asked Jesus to be our Saviour from sin and are seeking to make him the Lord of our lives, but we cannot be sure about others. Some of our friends may seem from the outside to be very nice, but what goes on in their hearts may be very different. There may be evil thoughts leading to evil words and deeds that we don't hear or see. So we are not to judge which are which, for we might be wrong. Besides, though the parable does not say so, the rest of Scripture makes clear that there is still time to change and 'those who are tares today may be wheat tomorrow'. You might explain briefly here how to change from being tares to wheat, or suggest that those people who want to know should ask you after the service.

However, one day there is going to be a great harvest festival – the greatest harvest festival ever. When will that be? Draw from the children 'End of World' and get the child holding that card to let the lower part down. When that day comes, and we cannot say when it will be, then it will be too late to change. Jesus will send his angel reapers to gather up the tares, and the lost will be separated from God for ever. Explain that these are not your words, but the words of the most loving and kind Person who ever lived. It is because he loves us so much that he has warned us this is going to happen. If someone knows that a part of the beach at the seaside is dangerous, it is an act of love and kindness to warn people. Jesus warns us that if we reject him and continue to follow the devil the result will be deadly serious. (Now make 'Field', 'Devil', 'Tares' and 'Harvest' sit down.) However, for all who follow Jesus he will gather the saved into his barn. Where is that? (Heaven.) Describe briefly what a wonderful place that will be for all who love Jesus Christ.

Note

This talk by Michael Botting has been adapted by kind permission of Scripture Union from the outline first published in *Teaching Juniors*, July–September 1966.

25. Take Root and Bear Fruit

Aim

To illustrate the Christian life by means of a fruitful tree.

Text

2 Kings 19:29–30.

Drama

Acting Up 'In the Beginning', Parts I and II; *50 Sketches for All Occasions* 15 'The Jam Factory'.

Hymns and songs

Select from Harvest section of church hymn book. 'I have a destiny' (SOF 212); 'You are the Vine' (SOF 629).

Prayers

400 Prayers 94, 107, 119, 274.

Main talk

Preparation

Get a good artist to paint on a large sheet of white cardboard a healthy-looking tree with its roots visible. Stick on the tree near the top, in the middle and near the bottom of the foliage, three fruit-like shapes, possibly in day-glo red. With a sharp Stanley-type blade cut out four rectangles each three to four inches wide and long enough for the four words *Jesus*, *repentance*, *Spirit* and *souls* printed on an under sheet of card to show through the gaps. One of the rectangles should be in the roots of the tree to reveal *Jesus* underneath. The other three should each carry one of the fruit and should be separated from the next by the same width as the rectangle width.

Have a good length of very thin nylon thread, which can be obtained from a shop selling angling equipment.

Make some holes in your cardboard, knot the thread at one end and thread about half an inch above the first gap. Bring the thread through the rectangle that has been cut out, about one inch top and bottom, and then thread it about one inch from the next rectangular space.

Proceed down the rectangles and up again on the other side. When the whole visual aid has been threaded, the effect will be that the pieces cut out can be raised and lowered and yet still remain part of the visual aid. (See also Talk 4.) Move the rectangles down to show words underneath as the talk unfolds.

Presentation

In a number of places in the Bible people are compared to trees (eg Psalm 1:3, Luke 3:9). Relate Isaiah's words to King Hezekiah concerning the house of Judah, who were told to 'take root downward and bear fruit upward'. Ask how this might apply to a Christian.

1. *Take root downward* Some trees can have incredibly deep and strong roots. Paul wrote to the Ephesians and Colossians that they should be rooted in Christ (Ephesians 3:17; Colossians 2:6). Reveal *Jesus* in the roots of the visual aid. Why Jesus? Speak about some current views of Jesus

which are usually contrary to the biblical picture, eg weak, superstar. Describe the Jesus of the gospels as tough, strong, courageous, as well as compassionate and loving. Refer to the cross, resurrection and ascension and our need to repent and believe in him. That is how we become rooted in Jesus.

If we have become rooted this should show itself in various ways, which brings us to the second part of our text.

2. *Bear fruit upward* The Bible refers to three ways in which we can bear fruit:

- *Fruit of repentance* (Matthew 3:8). John the Baptist stressed the need for evidence that repentance was real; that when we confessed our sins and asked God's forgiveness we really were sorry to God for our sins.
- *Fruit of the Spirit* (Galatians 5:22). Is not this the sort of fruit we all want to see around us in the lives of others, as well as ourselves? It can only happen as we receive Jesus and the gift of his Holy Spirit. The evidence that we really have done so is the fruit of the Spirit that other people see in us, just as the fruit all around us at our harvest festival is evidence of a lot of planting some time ago.
- *Fruit of souls* Refer to John 4:36 and Jesus' explanation that winning people for him was rather like a harvest. Paul in Romans 1:13 explains how he wanted to win some Roman souls for Christ. It should be the desire and ambition of every genuine Christian to want to win other souls for Jesus.

26. The Feast of Tabernacles

Aim

To use the Jewish Feast of Tabernacles to bring deeper understanding to our Christian harvest festivals.

Texts

Deuteronomy 16:13–17; John 8:12; 7:37–39.

Drama

There is a lot of action in the building of the tabernacle; additional drama should hardly be necessary. However, if thought desirable, see two suggestions in Talks 24 and 25.

Hymns and songs

Select from Harvest section in church hymn book. 'God is good' (SOF 132); 'Let your living water flow' (SOF 334); 'He made the earth' (SOF 756).

Prayers

400 Prayers 94, 107, 119, 274.

Main talk

Preparation

This talk is not for the accident-prone speaker without a reasonable imagination!

Allowing plenty of time, build in a prominent position, possibly on a small stage, a miniature tabernacle or booth. The structure can be two clothes horses, though it can be pointed out that the fourth side would normally be against a house wall. The main features should be plenty of fresh leaves, some citrus fruit like lemons, oranges and grapefruit and that the structure is open to the sky. You should have a candle in a holder and matches available.

If there is enough space at the front of the church erect the Teazlegraph board. Add the main headings below in a variety of colours, eg orange, red and green respectively. Pictures of a sheath of corn, a cross and a well for water, all with Velcro on the back, could also be available.

Presentation

Refer to the tabernacle and explain that the Feast of Tabernacles was one of the Hebrew (or Jewish) harvest festivals. Put the citrus fruit in a conspicuous position around the tabernacle, explaining that they are more common in Israel than our apples and pears. Mention that the tabernacle would be open to the sky, could be as big as 12 by 10 feet, or even seat 100. People sometimes lived in them for a week in October. Ask why God told the people to build tabernacles, and what they could mean to us as Christians. (If you use the Teazlegraph board put up the word *Tabernacle* at the top and then the first main heading.)

1. *Thanksgiving for harvest* Refer to the fruit and explain that the feast was really very similar to our harvest festival. It was a time of great joy, the temple treasury was refilled, good

things were shared out to the poor. (Place picture of sheaf of corn on board alongside heading.)

2. *Release from slavery* This feast was commanded by God from the time that the children of Israel came out of their slavery in Egypt and wandered in the wilderness for forty years, living in tents.

Ask in what way we are in slavery. Draw out that we are slaves to sin. Then ask how we are released from sin and speak of the cross. (Put up the cross opposite the heading.)

As the feast developed over the years, various customs became linked with it, and two are referred to in John's Gospel.

(a) *Light* – The great candelabra in the temple court of the women was lit to represent the fire in the wilderness which guided the children of Israel by night. These four great lights in the temple shone out over the city of Jerusalem. This was done every night, but not on the last night of the feast.

Suddenly, as the sun was setting, Jesus spoke out to all the people, aware of the gloom: 'I am the light of the world.'

Explain that he is the one to show us the way to God and guide us in our daily living. (Light the candle by the model tabernacle.)

3. *Praise for the gift of rain* This custom was not commanded by God, but grew up after the Exile and was utilised by Jesus on the last great day of the feast.

(b) *Water* – Refer to the procession of priests down to the pool of Siloam, all dressed in white robes, collecting water in golden vases and carrying them to the temple gates where the water would be poured out. They would sing 'With joy you will draw water from the wells of salvation' (Isaiah 12:3).

This was performed on seven days, but not on the eighth day. At the moment on the eighth day when it would have been done, Jesus stepped forward and offered better water than Siloam: 'If a man is thirsty, let him come to me and drink.' Explain briefly his meaning from John 7:37–39 concerning the Holy Spirit.

Refer to the much greater thankfulness for water in parts of the world like Israel, than in Britain. (Put up well alongside heading.) Just as the Hebrews came to give thanks for rain poured out on them by God at their Feast of Tabernacles, we should give God thanks that he has poured out his Spirit on all those who have received Jesus as Saviour from sin.

27. A Talk for Bible Sunday

Aim

To introduce to the congregation the true meaning of the word 'Bible', namely a very special library.

Text

Luke 24:25–49. This will need a brief introduction to explain its context before being read aloud.

Drama

50 Sketches for All Occasions 17 'The Trip of a Lifetime'.

Hymns and songs

'Jesus, Jesus, holy and anointed One' (SOF 293); 'Have you got an appetite?' (SOF 746); 'Jesus, restore to us again' (SOF 876).

Prayers

400 Prayers 8, 9, 70, 154, 155, 195, 225, 249, 251, 359, 372.

Main talk

Preparation

On an OHP acetate draw an outline of an open Bible.

Attach three strips of acetate to either side of this with the following words:

On the left: History   *On the right:*   Gospels & Acts
                 Poetry   Letters
                 Prophecy   Revelation

Presentation

Ask who belongs to a library. Which is the nearest library? After possibly getting answers about local buildings, direct the congregation to the fact that there are a number of libraries in the church, namely the Bibles.

Show the outline Bible on the OHP and draw out the different sections the Bible contains, flipping across the acetate strips as these are mentioned.

Conduct a brief Bible study on the passage read from Luke 24, encouraging the congregation to have Bibles open in front of them.

Ask the following questions, referring to the verses where the answers are to be found: What's the passage about? (v. 25–27, 44–47 – draw out the answers Jesus, cross, resurrection, repentance and forgiveness of sins) Who's it for? (v. 47 – draw out the answer 'for all the world') How's it spread? (v. 48 – draw out 'by believers')

Tell one or more of the following stories:

In 1536 William Tyndale was strangled and burnt at the stake for translating the Bible into English so that any simple ploughman could understand it. His translation became the basis of the Authorised (King James) Version.

Some 200 years ago a young girl, Mary Jones, saved up her pennies and walked thirty miles barefoot to buy a Bible for herself. This event helped towards the founding of the Bible Society, which prints millions of Bibles every year for worldwide distribution.

Over 120 years ago an eighteen-year-old Sunday school

teacher, Annie Marston, encouraged her class in Keswick to read the Bible each day of the week. This led to the founding of the Scripture Union, which actually began on 1st April 1879 – one of the wisest things to happen on All Fools' Day!

How should we react? Surely we should value these little libraries – that probably most of us own – all the more. Not just for themselves, but because their message can change our lives.

28. Remembrance Sunday: The Real War

Aim

To use Remembrance Sunday to alert people's attention to the spiritual war which still rages, but which has already been won.

Text

Ephesians 6:10–20.

Story

The naturalised Frenchman – see below.

Hymns and songs

'In heavenly armour' (SOF 237); 'We shall stand' (SOF 589); 'O Righteous God' (SOF 967); 'Onward Christian Soldiers' (HTC 532).

Prayers

400 Prayers 185, 200, 242, 352, 353.

Main talk

Preparation

Prepare a series of OHP acetates. There are admittedly a lot here, but bear in mind this can be a very well attended service.

1. The heading *The real enemy* and the words 'The spiritual forces of evil in the heavenly realms'. Depict the devil as a snake, Jesus on the cross, a sword with blood on it, a gun and a bomb exploding.

2. One acetate with three parts, the first the whole sheet, the second and third able to be flipped over from the left edge of the main sheet. The artwork as follows:

(a) The word *Powerful* and the text 'against the rulers . . . the . . . authorities . . . the powers of this dark world'. Depict Jesus being tempted in the wilderness to accept 'all the kingdoms of the world'.
(b) The word *Wicked* and the text 'spiritual forces of evil'. Depict gas chambers and words '6 million dead'. Depict a dead soldier and words '50 million died in World Wars One and Two'. 'Geneva Convention' crossed out.
(c) The word *Cunning* and the text 'the devil's schemes' with picture of an angel but showing a snake's tail.

  The following should each be in two parts.

3.

(a) Depict Jesus from the cross shouting, 'It is finished' and a cross lying on top of a large dead snake.
(b) A Frenchman with beret and striped jersey standing by a Union Jack on a pole and saluting.

4.

(a) A font and words from baptism service either in full or in part 'We should not be ashamed . . . to our lives' end'.
(b) A soldier in armour. Words 'truth', 'righteousness',

'peace'. Also an open Bible with a sword piercing through it so that the sharp end points towards the reader.

5.

(a) A manger, person in armour brandishing a sword, trumpets.
(b) The famous World War One call-up picture, a bugle.

Presentation

Ask what we are especially remembering today. Fill in briefly any important information omitted, such as the awfulness of war, tremendous loss of life and the fact that some are still alive and suffering from terrible disfigurement, etc. However, these two wars are an illustration of an even more terrible war that is still in progress. Ask for suggestions and refer to the above text that has already been read during the service, stressing verse 12. Let's think together about the *real* conflict.

1. *The real enemy* (acetate 1) Make reference to the devil in the Garden of Eden, and to Jesus in the wilderness, and the evil people who plotted the crucifixion. Give illustrations of evil, such as the story of David, Bathsheba and Uriah the Hittite. (Children from an early age know a lot about sex and probably need to grasp that its misuse is sinful.) Refer to the latest horror stories in the media. Then mention that none of us is safe from this enemy. We are often not 'in love and charity with neighbours'. We may not actually murder or commit adultery, but we have hateful and impure thoughts. (See Matthew 5:21–30.) Perhaps describe the apostle Paul's inner struggle (Romans 7:21–23). Mention a British general who once said, 'It is fatal to underestimate your enemy and make a small war.' We must not do the same.

Our enemy is *Powerful* (acetate 2a). Refer to Jesus in the wilderness. He is *Wicked* (acetate 2b). Mention that our spiritual enemies use their powers destructively. (We have already referred to the 6 million dying in gas chambers and 50 million in two World Wars.) They recognise no Geneva Convention. They hate the light, as we do when we give in to our temptations.

Our enemy is *Cunning* (acetate 2c). The devil likes either to disguise himself as an angel of light or, better still, to deceive people that he does not really exist:

> The devil they fair voted out,
> And of course the devil's gone.
> But simple folk would like to know –
> Who carries his business on?

We can be encouraged, however, because all is not lost. Christianity is good news. We can rejoice in:

2. *The real victory* State that unlike the two World Wars we remember today, where the victory was by no means certain, victory in the real war was settled long ago by Jesus on the cross. (Show acetate 3a and explain briefly the finished work of Christ.)

Tell the story of the Frenchman who became a naturalised Englishman. When asked what difference it had made he explained that whereas previously he had lost the Battle of Waterloo, now he had won it! (Acetate 3b.) Explain that when we accept Jesus as Saviour by repentance and faith, we transfer from being on the losing side of the devil to the winning side of Jesus.

3. *The real war* Although victory has been achieved, the war is not over. Evil spiritual forces are all around us, encouraging us to defect and become traitors to the Christian cause.

Refer to the need to take the statements made at our baptism seriously (show acetate 4a). But how? Comment on the Christian armour mentioned in text, as time allows (show acetate 4b). Only as we put on the whole spiritual armour will we be able to stand (v. 13).

4. *The real armistice* Paul begins our text with 'Finally', which has the meaning of 'henceforth' or 'for the remaining time'. He wants us to understand that from the first coming of Jesus, at the first Christmas, to his final coming at the end of the world, we have to be fighting in the spiritual war (acetate 5a). If we are not aware of this conflict it can only mean that we are on the wrong side, because the devil does not bother those who are still his own. We need to change sides by repenting of our sins and believing in Jesus.

For those who know the truth let today be a day to rouse ourselves to the spiritual fight (acetate 5b). There will be no cessation of hostilities, no temporary truce or cease-fire, until the end of life or history, when the real armistice is declared and eternal peace is ushered in.

Perhaps quote Revelation 3:21 and 21:4.

Has everyone here today joined up in the *real* war?

THE CHRISTIAN LIFE

29. An Anniversary Talk – In Jesus

Aim

To summarise the Christian faith by means of an elaborate visual aid that will be appreciated by all ages, based on an original idea of the late Dr Ernest Kevan, one time principal of London Bible College.

Text

2 Corinthians 5:17.

Drama

50 Sketches for All Occasions 24 'Home Improvements'.

Hymns and songs

'God forgave my sin' (SOF 129); 'I am a new creation' (SOF 197); 'I'm accepted' (SOF 229); 'Just as I am' (SOF 316); 'My lips shall praise You' (SOF 937).

Prayers

400 Prayers 4. The talk covers such a wide range of themes that the Index from page 181 of *400 Prayers* should be consulted.

Main talk

Preparation

Construct eight boxes of various sizes so that each fits into the other. It is only necessary to have four of the six sides of each box, as the back and the base are not visible to the congregation. The boxes can be quite easily constructed out of hardboard and stuck together with Bostick. The boxes should have on them in the following order, going from the largest to the smallest, 'Jesus', 'Sin' with a cross stuck across it, 'Power', 'Bible', 'Prayer' or praying hands, 'Church', 'Joy', 'Heaven'. The size of the boxes should be such that when placed on a table and built up with the smallest box at the top, the speaker is unable to put the last box up without standing on a chair or stool to do so. Convenient dimensions of the largest box could be – front face, height 12″, width 13″, depth of box 9¼″. The next box – front face 11½″, width 12½″, depth 9″, and the proportions of each box decreasing by the same amount each time. At the beginning of the talk the boxes should be packed one inside the other and covered with a black cloth.

Presentation

Refer to the fascination our grandparents or great grandparents seemed to have with cemeteries. Mention the statement on many tombstones: 'In Christ' or 'In Jesus'. Hence refer to the text.

What does it mean to be 'in Jesus'? Reveal the boxes with the first box showing the word 'Jesus'. Remove the box and place alongside the others to reveal 'Sin' crossed out and enlarge on how Christ's death on the cross made it possible for God to forgive (cancel) our sins.

Go on to reveal each of the boxes, gradually building them higher and higher as you talk on each subject. Before going on to the next box, recap by saying that to be 'in Jesus'

means sin forgiven, the power of the Holy Spirit, the Bible coming alive, prayer becoming real, the church becoming a fellowship and an inward joy even in the midst of trouble.

When you reach the final box, but before you show it, state that there is something different about this box from all the others. Whereas they refer to Christian experience in this life, the last refers to the Christian life after physical death. Hence reveal 'Heaven' and step up on the chair or stool to put the box on top.

Speak briefly about heaven and ask the congregation whether they can say they know the truth of these things because they are 'in Jesus'. You can either end the talk by packing all the boxes away and recapping as you do so or you can deliberately leave the boxes piled up as a reminder to the congregation as they leave the church.

30. What Does Baptism Mean?

Aim

To explain the meaning of baptism, preferably when a baptism is taking place during the service.

Text

Acts 16:16–34 (preferably read from the *Dramatised Bible*).

Hymns and songs

See section of church hymn book on Baptism. 'I believe in Jesus' (SOF 203); 'River, wash over me' (SOF 487); 'Wash me clean' (SOF 1074).

Prayers

400 Prayers 56. In Index see under Family general and Home. The Baptism Service itself will also include prayers.

Main talk

Preparation

Have the words 'Forgiveness', 'Faith', 'Fight', 'Family' and 'Fun' ready to be revealed at the appropriate moment as you tell the story of the Philippian jailer. The words could be made of fluorescent paper stuck onto five pieces of rectangular black card, different coloured paper being used for each word, or you could have them on an acetate to be used on an OHP.

Presentation

There are several references in the New Testament to family baptisms. For example, Cornelius, the Roman soldier, was converted to Jesus Christ and he and all his family were baptised.

What is baptism? It is a visible sign of something that is difficult to put into words. We use signs for lots of things. A kiss is a sign of love, a salute is a sign of loyalty, and a handshake is a sign of friendship. At a wedding the bride and groom give each other rings to wear as a sign that they are married.

What does baptism mean? Let us look at another story in Acts where a baptism takes place. Briefly tell the story of the Philippian jailer. Put up the word cards or acetates making the following points:

1. *Forgiveness* The jailer was a sinner. He needed salvation, including the forgiveness of his sins (v. 31). The reason why water is used in baptism is because it illustrates the washing away of sin.

2. *Faith* The jailer had to have faith in the Lord Jesus (v. 31), the one who had died for his sins on the cross.

3. *Fight* The Christian life is not easy. It is a fight. Paul and Silas were beaten and thrown into prison because of their witness to Jesus (vv. 22–24).

4. *Family* But to be a Christian means that you are welcomed into a new family. Reference could be made to the church that had begun in the house of Lydia.

5. *Fun* Finally, the Christian life is also fun. For all their trials and troubles the apostles and the jailer and his household rejoiced (vv. 25 and 34).

If a baptism is actually to take place, appropriate parts of the service can be quoted to illustrate the above points, eg on 'Fight' – 'valiantly as a disciple of Christ'.

31. Red Alert! Christian Victory

Aim

To show that the Bible offers us, through Christ, victory over the spiritual forces of evil.

Text

Ephesians 6:10–18.

Drama

Acting Up 'In the Beginning', Part II only, pp. 9–10; *50 Sketches for All Occasions* 8 'Nailed!'.

Hymns and songs

'Blessed be the name of the Lord' (SOF 46); 'Fight the good fight'; 'Our confidence is in the Lord' (SOF 452); 'Rejoice, rejoice!' (SOF 480).

Prayers

400 Prayers 35, 62, 200, 208, 373.

Main talk

Preparation

This talk, when originally given in St George's Hall, Bradford, at the Northern Pathfinder and CYFA Rally, followed a very vivid dramatic presentation of the forces of evil being overcome through the power of Christ. It was illustrated by suitable pictures on an overhead projector. Anyone using this talk outline should therefore obtain the services of a good artist who can illustrate the talk as liberally as possible.

Presentation

1. We are all engaged in a real battle, because this wonderful world which God has made for us to enjoy has been invaded by an evil power totally opposed to God and anything good. It all began in heaven when Satan dared to make himself like the Most High God. Then Satan lied to Eve and made her think that God was keeping something back from her. So she fell into sin and Adam, her husband, did too.

2. When God sent Jesus into the world to save us from our sins, Satan tried to get rid of him. Refer to the slaying of the innocents at the first Christmas, and Jesus' temptations in the wilderness and the Garden of Gethsemane. However, Jesus did not avoid going to the cross, where he died for our sins and cried from the cross the great words of victory, '*It is finished!*' He was totally victorious over the powers of evil and Satan was vanquished. The following resurrection and ascension were all part of the evidence.

3. Although Satan is ultimately beaten, yet he is still around fighting a last ditch stand and doing his best to disrupt this world and prevent men and women, boys and girls following Jesus. War, famine, crime, mugging and ouija boards are all evidence that Satan is still alive and well and living on planet earth.

BEWARE! You and I are not going to take much notice of Satan all the time we think of him as a big joke – someone who runs around in red tights, has horns and carries a three-pronged fork. Deception is his business, and he is no better pleased than when he convinces people he does not exist. He lied to Eve and he will to us, especially by suggesting that God is keeping good things back from us and that the path to life can be found through drink, drugs, sex and the occult.

Satan also sows big doubts about Jesus. Should we fall into sin, though he is the tempter, he will jeer at us and say, 'Call yourself a Christian and you behave like that!' He is very fond of appearing like a roaring lion, so that we are scared to stand up for Jesus, as Peter was when his master was arrested. Actually, a lion is least dangerous when it roars; it is the hunting lion that is quiet.

What are the secrets of victory?

- *We must be on the victory side.* Tell the story of the Frenchman who became a naturalised Englishman. When asked what difference it made he replied that whereas previously he had lost the Battle of Waterloo, now he had won it! When we join Jesus' side, we enter into his victory.
- *We must live the victory life.* Enlarge on the need to put self on the cross. (See *The Message of Galatians* by John R. W. Stott, IVP, pp. 150–2, for a particularly helpful treatment of this subject.) Then deal with the need for Bible reading, prayer, the church, worship, witness and the power of the Holy Spirit. End with promise in Revelation 3:21.

32. Think No Evil

Aim

To teach that evil thoughts are just as sinful in God's eyes as evil actions, and one can easily lead to the other.

Text

Matthew 5:21–28.

Drama

50 Sketches for All Occasions 1 'Lead Us Not Into . . .' might be adapted and used towards the end of the talk.

Hymns and songs

'Purify my heart' (SOF 475); 'When I look into Your holiness' (SOF 595); 'Don't let my love grow cold' (SOF 702); 'Take my life and let it be' (HTC 554).

Prayers

400 Prayers 30, 203, 217, 370, 371, 407.

Main talk

Preparation

Using long strips of Velcro (which can always be used later

for other Teazlegraph talks) make an outline of an iceberg on the Teazlegraph board. Only about a seventh is showing above light blue velcro representing the sea surface.

Have the words *MURDER* and *ADULTERY* on strips of card covered with Teazle material.

Using different coloured day-glo card draw four pictures representing *hate* (red card with a dagger), *anger* (orange card with a springing tiger), *envy* (green card with weeds) and *lust* (pink card with semi-clad figure). The four words can be worked into pictures.

Have the word *SIN* on a piece of card, and a red cross to go across it; a flame to represent the Holy Spirit and a face with lines on the forehead to suggest thought. Each should be backed with Velcro. The visuals can also be done on OHP.

Presentation

(Show the outline of the iceberg and ask for ideas of what it might be. Ascertain that only a small proportion of the iceberg is visible above the surface of the sea.) Today we are going to think about two of God's commandments: not to murder or commit adultery. (Place the two words above the sea surface.)

Murder means to deliberately kill for personal gain. Adultery is an umbrella term for any misuse of our sexual instincts. Now if you were to ask how many here had broken either of these commandments probably no one would own up, because probably no one literally had. However, what if you were to ask how many had *thought* about either . . .? We say, 'If looks could kill . . .' or 'I wish you were dead.' That is why we are calling this talk 'Think no evil'.

Now ask why we have an iceberg on the board, and draw out that thoughts are invisible below the surface, but do occasionally appear in actions. Evil thoughts can lead to evil actions. For instance:

1. *Hate* (Put *hate* visual in iceberg under sea surface.) Refer to the hatred of the religious leaders in Jesus' day which led to murder. Religious people have at times put one another to death; for instance during the Reformation and in Ireland today. Nursing hate can ruin our lives and if we cannot forgive someone then God says he cannot forgive us.

2. *Anger* (Read Matthew 5:22.) Explain how a tiger suddenly pounces. Cain killed Abel because of anger. Jesus tells us we must make up our quarrels quickly, and Paul says that the sun should never set on our wrath.

3. *Envy* Envy was responsible for the worst crime in history (Matthew 27:18). This sin can be rather like a weed that keeps coming up despite uprooting, smothering, poisoning. It works underground and then suddenly comes to the surface in a disgraceful word or action. We can be envious of people's possessions, jobs, gifts, homes, skill at games, even their apparent success in Christian work. Envy can grow in us all: children, housewives, school-teachers, doctors – even ministers of religion!

4. *Lust* (Read Matthew 5:27–28.) Make it clear this can have nothing to do with enjoying the sight of a pretty girl or handsome man, or else no marriage would ever be a love match (not of the romantic kind, anyway). Jesus is quite clear that this refers to allowing the mind to dwell on impure thoughts, which can lead to the misuse of sex.

This will mean that we must be careful what books we read, films or TV plays we watch and websites we visit. Perhaps mention the story of David and Bathsheba, and that horrific murders have arisen through the reading of pornography. The Bible teaches that the only right use of sex is in the context of marriage. God invented it and planned it for our good.

How do we deal with evil thoughts that can lead to evil actions?

- Confess as soon as we fall into sinful thought. Refer to texts like Proverbs 28:13, Psalm 32:1–5, the stories of David and Bathsheba or the woman taken in adultery. Put up the visual of *SIN* covered by the cross.
- Ask the Holy Spirit to help us set our minds upon him (Romans 8:5–6). Put up visual of the flame.
- Point out the need for positive and pure thinking (Philippians 4:8). Put up visual of the face. 'Think about these things.'

33. Don't Worry!

Aim

To teach members of the church family the futility of being anxious.

Text

Matthew 6:25–34.

Drama

50 Sketches for All Occasions 43 'The Qualm Before the Storm'.

Hymns and songs

'Be bold, be strong' (SOF 37); 'You are my hiding place' (SOF 625); 'Quiet my mind, Lord' (SOF 983); 'Jesus, lover of my soul' (HTC 438); 'We trust in you, our shield and our defender' (HTC 446).

Prayers

400 Prayers 223, 231.

Main talk

Preparation

Use the Teazlegraph board and prepare strips to be placed on it with the following words: *worry is, senseless, needless*

137

and faithless. Also have some simple cut-outs of a bird, flower, some food and clothes with Velcro on the back. Alternatively use an OHP.

Presentation

Whatever age we are we can be tempted to worry: school, exams, games, illness, unemployment, the children, money, clothes, food, a house, death . . . the list is endless. If you do not believe in God and have never committed your life to Jesus Christ, then there is nothing more to be said. Life is meaningless and you are a puppet in the hand of blind chance. You have good reason to worry. I would!

But if you really are a Christian, then Jesus has a very clear message for you: 'Don't worry!' In our lesson (assuming it has been read during the service) Jesus says five times we should not be anxious – that is, we should not worry – and gives three reasons why we shouldn't. (Put up at the top of the Teazlegraph board *worry is*, then on the left-hand side put the other three words as you come to speak about them.)

1. *Worry is senseless (v.25)* God gave us bodies and life; we could do nothing about that so surely we can trust him to feed and clothe us (v.26). Jesus says, '*Your* heavenly Father feeds them', ie the birds who cannot call God their Father. If he looks after them, how much more we can be sure he will look after us. Put up the bird opposite the word *senseless* (v.27). We cannot lengthen our span of life, but worry might well shorten it.

2. *Worry is needless (vv.28–30)* God clothes the lily, or any flower for that matter, which only lasts for a short while, yet so magnificently as to outshine the glory of Solomon. Surely he can and will look after us who are his children. (Put up the flower opposite the word *needless*.)

3. *Worry is faithless (vv.30–33)* Stress 'men of little faith'. To be constantly worried about food, drink and clothes shows lack of faith in our heavenly Father. This is not saying that these things do not matter, but they should not totally absorb us. To worry is to behave like Gentiles, that is like those who do not believe. All around us there are lots of people whose lives are dominated by food and drink and clothes. (Put up pictures on board opposite the word *faithless*.) But we Christians have a far greater and more important concern – the kingdom of God.

End with a story of someone who really did exercise wonderful faith and God so obviously provided for his or her needs. Gladys Aylward or former 'Wiretapper' Jim Vaus are especially good examples. Perhaps some of you here are thinking, 'Oh, but things like that just don't happen in my life.' Have you ever given God a chance?

34. Cheer Up!

Aim

To teach that the surest way to real happiness is by receiving the gospel.

Text

Matthew 9:1–7.

Drama

50 Sketches for All Occasions 24 'Home Improvement'.

Hymns and songs

'Come on and celebrate' (SOF 73); 'Jesus put this song into our hearts' (SOF 299); 'I could sing unending songs' (SOF 790); 'Rejoice, the Lord is King' (HTC 180).

Prayers

400 Prayers (forgiveness) 28, 388, 405; (freedom) 4, 57, 397; (faith) 3, 46, 70, 202, 218.

Main talk

Preparation

This talk was originally shown on Yorkshire Television. An

artist in the congregation painted three pictures illustrating the text: four men carrying the sick man on a stretcher, Jesus leaning over the sick man, and the man standing upright holding his stretcher and looking radiantly happy. I also had the words *forgiveness*, *freedom*, and *faith* on Teazle-covered strips of card, and the word *sin* with a red day-glo cross to go across it, two heart shapes in red and pink day-glo card and two flame shapes in red and orange day-glo card. The hearts and flames were fixed together in pairs so that part of the pairs could be seen behind the other. All the visuals had Velcro stuck on the back. Make appropriate adaptations of the above if using an OHP.

Presentation

Ask how people are feeling today. Suggest problems that may be making them worried or unhappy. You could hardly be worse off than the man we heard about in the reading. He was paralysed, with no National Health Service or social security. Put up on left-hand side of Teazlegraph board the picture of the men carrying the stretcher and under it the man lying on the ground with Jesus looking over him.

When friends of the sick man brought him to Jesus he said to him 'Take heart' or 'Cheer up'. (These words could also be put at the top of the board if there is room.) Ask 'So what?' Explain that Jesus went to the heart of the problem, which was *sin*. Put the word on the right-hand side of the board at the same level as the lower picture. Jesus said, 'Your sins are forgiven.' Some people might think he was missing the point. But things have not changed. The cause of the world's problems, and yours and mine individually, is the human heart, out of which, said Jesus, come evil thoughts, theft, murder, adultery, coveting. What then is Jesus' remedy for cheering us up?

1. *Faith* Perhaps you are saying that forgiveness and freedom

are just what you want, but you want to know how to get them. Refer to the four men who brought the sick man to Jesus. It was when Jesus saw their faith that he was able to act. (Put up *faith* opposite the top picture and the two hearts on the right-hand side of the board.) Explain faith in terms of trust and exhort congregation to cheer up.

2. *Forgiveness* (Put up the word between the second picture and the word *sin*.) What right had Jesus to offer the sick man forgiveness, the religious leaders quite rightly asked, since God is the only one who can forgive sin? Explain that when we sin we often hurt other people, but supremely God. David quite rightly admitted in Psalm 51 after sinning over Bathsheba and Uriah the Hittite that it was against God that he had sinned. But how can God forgive when he has expressly said that the soul that sins must die? The answer lies in Jesus.

Enlarge on his primarily coming to earth to be the Saviour of mankind, mentioning the name he was given at his birth, and the cancelling of sin on the cross on the first Good Friday. (Place the red cross across the word *sin* on the board.) The evidence that Jesus had the right to tell the man his sins were forgiven was that he had the power to make him get up and walk.

3. *Freedom* (Put up the third picture under the second and the word *freedom* alongside.) Just as Jesus was able to free the man from his sickness so he could free him and us from sin. He did this by sending us his Holy Spirit, after ascending to his Father in heaven. (Put up the tongues of fire alongside *freedom*.) Ask what this really means. Not freedom to do as I like, but freedom to do what I should. Perhaps illustrate with a graphic story of someone freed from sin through Christ.

35. Take and Give

Aim

To show that giving should take place in two directions – we must receive from God but also give to him. Can be adapted for a special gift day, a baptism, harvest or Christmas.

Text

2 Corinthians 9:15.

Drama

50 Sketches for All Occasions 19 'Giving'.

Hymns and songs

'At this time of giving' (SOF 33); 'God forgave my sin' (SOF 129); 'I, the Lord of sea and sky' (SOF 830); 'Take my life and let it be'.

Prayers

400 Prayers 206, 212, 378.

Main talk

Preparation

Find or make four boxes that fit into each other with reasonable ease. Cover the largest with gold paper and mark on it on different sides the word 'LIFE' and symbols to represent forgiveness (the word 'sin' with a cross over it) and the Holy Spirit (tongues of fire). The second box should be covered in silver paper and have symbols on it representing money, such as a £ sign and seven-sided coin with 50 in it. The third box could have pink day-glo paper on it with symbols representing different talents or abilities, such as music, sport, cooking, carpentry, etc. The smallest box should also be covered in bright paper and have a clock face on it. At the start of the talk all the boxes should be inside one another, so that only the largest is visible.

Also have two pieces of card, preferably red day-glo, 3″ or 8 cm in width, and in length one 2′9″ or 84 cm and the other 1′6″ or 46 cm. With black lettering 2½″ or 7 cm high and 1½″ or 4 cm wide, put the word 'GENEROUSLY' on the longer strip vertically and the letters 'LOVI GLY' on the other strip horizontally. The two strips should then be joined with the shorter behind the longer with a suitable fastener, so that initially only the latter is visible, but when the smaller is turned into view, the word LOVINGLY appears, because the 'N' does service for both words, and the whole shape becomes a cross.

Presentation

Ask who likes birthdays. Whose is the greatest? Why do we like such occasions? Encourage the word 'present' or 'gift' to be mentioned and so introduce the text. What was God's priceless gift? Why is Jesus so important? Refer to John 3:16 and talk about the gift of eternal life, which we receive when we receive him as Saviour. Reveal your parcel and enlarge on the particular gifts of forgiveness and the Holy Spirit made possible through Jesus, showing the sides of the largest parcel. Ask the congregation if they have received God's priceless gift of Jesus and explain how. Parts of the baptism service can be quoted to help make these points.

However, when we receive gifts, we should normally be so grateful that we want to respond by giving in return, as a kind of 'thank you'. But what gifts do we have to offer God? Draw out from the congregation the following three ways, helped by the illustrations on the boxes, and comment appropriately:

- Possessions, especially money. If parts of 2 Corinthians 8–9 have been read during the service, suitable parts could be quoted.
- Abilities.
- Time.

How should we give? Draw out from 2 Corinthians 9:6–7 the words 'GENEROUSLY' and 'LOVINGLY', and show the cross with those words on it. Finally, quote 2 Corinthians 8:9 and 9:15.

36. Work, Rest and Worship

Aim

To teach the proper stewardship of time.

Text

Mark 6:30–46.

Drama

50 Sketches for All Occasions 21 'Remember Your Creator'.

Hymns and songs

'From the rising of the sun' (SOF 121); 'I want to serve the purpose of God' (SOF 260); 'Standing in Your presence' (SOF 1011); 'Dear Lord and Father of mankind' (HTC 356).

Prayers

400 Prayers 50, 75, 126, 127, 133, 134, 199, 236.

Main talk

Preparation

Design visuals for the Teazlegraph board, each backed with Velcro, of a clock face, a calendar, and a circular disc with each quarter a different colour to represent the seasons, such as green for spring, yellow for summer, buff for autumn and white for winter. Also have visuals to represent *work*, such as a spade or fork; *rest*, such as a bat and ball or a CD; and worship, such as figures with uplifted arms, an open Bible and praying hands. The three nouns that form the title of this talk should be on strips of Teazle-covered card. Make appropriate adaptation of the above if using an OHP

Presentation

You are thinking about a very strange thing. We all have been promised just so much, but some will have more, others less. All of us will use up the same amount by the end of this service. Here are some illustrations of it. (Put up clock face, calendar and seasons disc.) By now someone should have mentioned 'time'.

Go on to say that God has made us responsible for how we use it and ask what should be included in our use of time. Mention with texts, sleeping (Psalm 3:5), working (Genesis 2:15), eating (Genesis 2:16), exercising (1 Timothy 4:8), worshipping (Luke 4:16) and resting (Mark 6:31).

God intended us especially to do three things. (Put up visuals alongside three main words as you proceed with the talk.)

1. *Work (Mark 6:31b)* God is a worker and made us in his image. Jesus was a carpenter and preacher. Paul was a tentmaker and taught the importance of work. Work is one of the ways in which we can serve and glorify God, quite apart from bringing us pay and often much pleasure. Because of sin, however, much work is hard. Refer to the problem of unemployment, which the Bible sees as a sign of God's judgement (Zechariah 8:10). Jesus' parable of the labourers in the vineyard suggests there has always been unemployment, and probably always will be till he returns. Out-of-work Christians should be encouraged to be involved in

voluntary work, of which there is an enormous amount to be done.

2. *Rest (Mark 6:31a)* God has worked into our lives proper time for rest. Refer to the clock, calendar and seasons disc and explain about the need to rest each day, take a day off each week and a holiday in the year, perhaps explaining how even the earth rests through the pattern of the seasons. Reference can be made to the failure of the French experiment to get more work out of people by trying a ten day week. Mention the folly of working seven days a week and doing homework on Sundays.

3. *Worship (Luke 4:16; Mark 6:46)* The Sabbath was also designed for worship and God obviously intends that we should include it in our use of time, mainly in two ways: worshipping together as we are now, and also spending time with him daily in private Bible reading and prayer.

Conclude by telling the well-known story, perhaps apocryphal, of Henry Ford helping a driver of one of his cars. He designed the car, so knew how it worked best. The Bible is God's handbook for human maintenance, which should include work, rest and worship.

Eddy Stride, one-time Rector of Spitalfields in East London, tells of a boy who had tatooed on his shoulders *'Death before employment'*. 'Anyone who works is a nut!' he said. Later, out of sheer boredom, he got work in a pre-cast concrete factory and was thrilled by it. God knows best.

Do our lives have a right balance of work, rest and worship?

37. Life's So Unfair. . .

Aim

To teach from Jesus' controversial parable that none of us can demand rights from God, but his grace is our salvation.

Text

Matthew 20:1–16, which could be read dramatically. Also prepare people to read the following verses during the talk: Philippians 4:11–13; 1 Peter 2:22–24.

Drama

50 Sketches for All Occasions 37 'The Queue'.

Hymns and songs

'Ascribe greatness' (SOF 26); 'Faithful One, so unchanging' (SOF 89); 'Only by grace' (SOF 441); 'Rock of Ages, cleft for me' (HTC 444).

Prayers

400 Prayers (on jealousy) 208, 227; (on grace) 71, 253, 371.

Main talk

Preparation

Prepare a series of OHP acetates as follows:

1. The words 'It's not fair . . .!' Under them a rough sketch of the outside of a modern facade of a Jobcentre.
2. Wealthy-looking person carrying Bible, and destitute pauper.
3. Aeroplane with words 'Forewarned is forearmed', and in small letters underneath ROYAL OBSERVER CORPS.
4. A picture representing the devil.
5. The words 'They demanded their *rights*' and a pair of traditional scales with the world weighing down one side and *God's love* in a heart shape in the upper pan.
6. The words 'They kept . . .' with a jar of ink and a quill pen sticking out and accounts on a scroll with 12 hours, 9, 6, 3, 1, one under another. (Acetates 5 and 6 could be paired, the former being at the top of a sheet and the latter being on half a sheet attached to the lower left-hand edge and being flipped over when required.)
7. The words 'They grumbled – see Philippians 4:11–13.'
8. The words 'They were . . .' and the picture of a face, completely green except for the hair and eye space. (Acetates 7 and 8 could be paired similarly to 5 and 6.
9. The words placed down the left-handside of the acetate: 'They accused the owner of injustice.'
10. A picture of Jesus hanging from the cross and the text at the bottom 1 Peter 2:22–24.

Presentation

Ask whether anyone has said or thought this recently at school, home or work. (Acetate 1 on OHP screen.) Even if the parable of the labourers has been read as the Lesson, briefly recap the story and point out that the money mentioned would be roughly a fair day's wage for a labourer to keep him and his family alive for a day. The first labourers agreed to this. The later labourers agreed to no fixed amount, but trusted the owner would pay a fair wage.

1. *Life does not seem fair* (acetate 2). Point out that we live in a world where there seems to be great unfairness. Some, like most of us here, have food, homes and money to spare and we have heard about the Lord Jesus. Others have none of these things (perhaps refer to the latest TV pictures of starving millions, flood victims etc.)
(a) If we don't believe in God there is no point in complaining that life's unfair, because there is no one to whom we can complain.
(b) If we do believe, then there is the real problem of envy, and two Psalms warn of this – 37 and 73 (perhaps quote bits). The Royal Observer Corps, which did so much to help win the Battle of Britain in 1940, have as their motto 'Forewarned is forearmed' (acetate 3). We need to be aware that a very busy devil will do his best to make us envious (acetate 4).

2. *Those complaining workers* Make the following points fairly briefly:
(a) *They demanded their rights* (acetate 5) and got them, namely a fair day's wage, whereas the others trusted God and discovered him loving and gracious.
(b) *They kept accounts* (acetate 6). Why should those who only worked one hour get the same? In fact those who had the shorter hours would no doubt have been pleased to work longer had they been given the chance, and they still had the same needs, namely themselves and their family to keep.

(The author confesses to his shame that he remembers privately complaining in his heart that he had all the work to do preparing for a televised Family Service, whereas others taking part had very little to do, yet he and they all got the same fees. He knew he should have been pleased, for his stipend was greater than theirs, but initially he wasn't!)

(c) *They grumbled* (acetate 7). Mention how God was not pleased with the Children of Israel when they did the same. By contrast, listen to how the apostle Paul reacted when he was quite unfairly put in prison. Have Philippians 4:11–13 read here.

(d) *They were jealous*. Put on acetate 8 and ask what the congregation think it means. Refer to Miriam in the Old Testament and the Prodigal's elder brother in the New Testament as other examples of jealousy. Point out what a fruitless sin jealousy is. We can get some pleasure from pride or lust, but jealousy brings no pleasure. It does not help our situation and it discourages God's grace towards us.

(e) *They accused the owner of injustice* (acetate 9). Refer to the woman of uncertain age who demanded of her photographer justice. To which he replied that it was not justice she needed but mercy! These men were quite wrong, because they got justice, namely exactly what had been agreed. Place acetate 10 on the screen and have 1 Peter 2:22–24 read.

You could finish with the story of John Charles Ryle, an Oxford cricket Blue. Anticipating a First in his degree, he sauntered late into Morning Prayer one Sunday early in 1838 just in time to hear the Second Lesson from Ephesians 2 being read with an air of the most impressive earnestness, especially the eighth verse – '*For by grace . . . are ye saved . . . through faith . . . and that . . . not of yourselves . . . it is the gift of God.*' Not till that moment, for all his classical scholarship and other attainments, had he ever rightly grasped the gospel of grace and salvation. Later he went on to become the first Bishop of Liverpool. The story can be found in *John Charles Ryle 1816–1900* by Marcus L. Loane (James Clarke, 1953, pp. 13–14).

Does everyone here know the grace of God that Ryle found?

38. The Lighthouse

Aim

To illustrate how Christians should witness to their faith by life and lip.

Text

Matthew 5:16.

Drama

50 Sketches for All Occasions 38 'All These Years'; *Scenes and Wonders* 'The Reluctant Evangelist', p. 59.

Hymns and songs

'I am a lighthouse' (SOF 196); 'Lord, the light of Your love is shining' (SOF 362); 'One shall tell another' (SOF 439); 'Men of Faith' (SOF 921).

Prayers

400 Prayers 5, 51, 52, 65, 149, 196, 255.

Main talk

Preparation.

Make the following four OHP acetates:

154

1. A traditional seaside lighthouse.

2. Yellow beams fixed to the above acetate so that they can be flipped across at the appropriate moment to give the impression that the lighthouse is shining.

3. The words 'lip' and 'life' in a dark colour, which are also attached to the first acetate, and which can be flipped across in turn to land on the beams from the lighthouse.

4. This is optional and could either fit as part of the first acetate or be completely separate. Ships seen being guided through dangerous rocks by the aid of the lighthouse beams.

Presentation

Talk about a holiday by the seaside where you have seen a lighthouse. Explain that Christians should be like lighthouses. Show your first OHP acetate and ask questions along the following lines:

1. *What is the purpose of a lighthouse?* Suggest: to decorate the seaside, somewhere for the keeper to live or show people around. You will probably get the answer 'to warn ships of danger', but do not accept that answer to your present question. Only accept the answer 'to give light'. Then ask what people are for. Suggest: to be amused, to live for themselves, to make a name for themselves, to earn lots of money. Get everyone to turn to Matthew 5:16 and draw out the answer 'to give light'.

2. *How does a lighthouse give light?* Does my lighthouse look as if it has light in it? Answer 'No'. Explain that light has to be put in and it has to be in touch with power, but it's dark there now. Are people born with light inside? No. They may look nice on the outside but they are dark inside. Enlarge on sin and our inability to keep God's law. People have to have light brought in. Where do people get their light from? Ask people to look up John 8:12. Explain how we have to receive

Jesus, the Light of the World, into our lives if we are going to be able to shine for him in the world.

3. *Does the lighthouse just keep the light inside, so that people can see round and the lighthouse keeper can read his newspaper?* Draw out the answer that the lighthouse must shine out. Flip on the OHP beams. Ask what else we must do, apart from asking Jesus to be our Saviour. Draw out that we must shine for him. Ask how we do that, and encourage the answer that we must show we are Christians by our life and lip. Flip these OHP acetates on.

4. *Why must a lighthouse shine?* Suggest: so that everyone can see what a wonderful lighthouse it is? No. Draw out: to warn ships of the danger of rocks and help them find the harbour. (Possibly put up OHP acetate 4.) Why must we shine out? To warn others that they must not live without Jesus Christ, but discover his love and forgiveness and glorify God by their lives lived for him.

39. The Early Church at Prayer

Aim

To encourage the congregation to realise that the early church was just as human as we are when it comes to prayer, but that does not excuse us from faithful praying. The full use of OHP visuals is recommended.

Text

Acts 12:1–19.

Drama

50 Sketches for All Occasions 49 'Peter, Prison and Prayer'.

Hymns and songs

'O Lord, hear my prayer' (SOF 423); 'O Lord, the clouds are gathering' (SOF 429); 'I lift my eyes to the quiet hills' (SOF 804).

Prayers

400 Prayers 202, 402.

Main talk

Preparation

Prepare the following OHP acetates:

1. The four in figure 1, each being placed on the OHP as indicated below. In the case of Peter, have him seated in prison alone, with the guard able to be separately flipped over and the '16 x' also able to be flipped over.

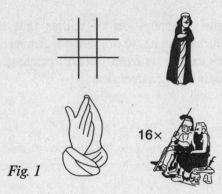

Fig. 1

2. See figure 2. 'Serious' should have only the upper parts of the arms showing, to be joined by the remainder of the bodies when 'Corporate' is reached. 'Specific' should be separate, and ready simply to be laid on the OHP.

Fig. 2

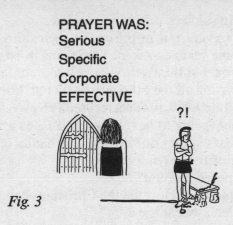

PRAYER WAS:
Serious
Specific
Corporate
EFFECTIVE

Fig. 3

3. A whole acetate as indicated in figure 3.

Presentation

Using the crisscross frame in figure 1, hold a quiz on Acts 12:
1–19, having read the passage (possibly dramatically). The
questions could be:

1. Who was leader of the early Christians?
2. Can you name another important leader mentioned in
   the story?
3. What happened to him?
4. By whom? (In speaking of Herod's soldiers, put the
   figure of Herod on the OHP and mention that this
   Herod's father was the one before whom Jesus came at
   the time of his trial. His grandfather had had the babies
   around Bethlehem killed at the time of the first
   Christmas.)
5. What happened to Peter? Put him on OHP.
6. Was he alone? Add one soldier. Any more? Add '16 x'.
   Comment that it would seem the Christians must have
   been seen as very powerful for Herod to take such
   serious action, namely the deepest part of the prison,

probably 16 soldiers, chains and sentries.

    People are still put in prison for their faith in Jesus Christ. Some years ago some Christians in Nepal were put in prison, but they were soon released, because they were converting all the other prisoners to Christ!

7. When the church in Jerusalem realised Peter was in prison and probably going to be tortured and killed at the next festival, what did they do? Put 'praying hands' on OHP.
8. Name one of the praying group.
9. What happened to Peter?
10. (Reserve question) How did the Christians behave when first told Peter was at the door?

At the end of the quiz clear the OHP and suggest that we think a little more about the prayer of that group:

1. *It was serious* (v. 5 'earnestly praying' – OHP arms in air). The situation was desperate and there was nothing they could do humanly speaking, but they could pray, and did.

    Their praying is compared to the earnest praying of Jesus in the Garden of Gethsemane, fervent and continuous. It needed to be, because Peter's death was imminent.

    How seriously do we take prayer? We recognise the importance of getting out of the way of ambulances and fire-engines to save physical life, but do we have the same concern for those dying spiritually? Especially what effort do we make to pray?

2. *It was specific* (v. 5 'for him', that is for Peter – OHP). They named their need very precisely. Perhaps refer to the parable on prayer in Luke 11:5, where the man is very specific about what he requires from his neighbour, namely three loaves. In our prayers we should name names and needs, not just ask God to bless everybody.

3. *It was corporate* (v. 5 'the church was earnestly praying' OHP join up arms with bodies). There is a place for our private prayers, but Scripture seems to teach that there is special power when we gather together to pray about matters on which we agree.

4. *It was effective* (clear the OHP and place third acetate on). Peter was freed. Let us be encouraged that despite their partial faith God acted.

The God they prayed to is also our God. It is not a question of great faith in God, but faith in a great God.

Summarise the four headings and pray.

BIBLICAL CHARACTERS AND MISCELLANEOUS TALKS

40. The Creation of Humanity

Aim

To think about the wonder of humanity's creation.

Text

Genesis 2:4–25.

Drama

Acting Up 'In the Beginning' Part I, pp. 7–9.

Hymns and songs

'I lift my eyes up' (SOF 221); 'I will praise You all my life' (SOF 272); 'He made the earth' (SOF 756); 'I'll praise my maker while I've breath' (HTC 20).

Prayers

400 Prayers 1, 195, 302.

Main talk

Preparation

Have the seven headings below on Teazlegraph strips ready to place on a Teazlegraph board (or use an OHP), and also a picture of an ape. Conceal a man lying under a blanket near where you give the talk. Also have a piece of coal, some chalk, a cellar of salt, a glass of water, a portable musical instrument, a painting and a garden fork. Ask the organist to be ready to play the opening bars of some stirring music. Have a sign-post with 'right' and 'wrong' on it.

Presentation

Ask in what section of a library the congregation would expect to find the Bible or books about it: religion or science? Explain that religion is for all time and must be put across so that the simplest of people can understand it. It explains, or should do, the purpose of man in the world. Science, on the other hand, attempts to explain *how* the world works. Today, as we think about our creation, we are not going to say if our first parents looked like this (show picture of an ape), but see what the Bible says about what sort of creation God made man to be. God gave man:

1. *A body* (v. 7a). We are dust from the ground. Produce the coal, chalk, salt and water and explain that that is what we are chiefly made of, valued at a few pounds. *Adam* is the Hebrew word for ground from which man came and gets his name. Reveal the lifeless man lying on the ground, and explain that a lifeless body is no use, but only fit to be put back into the ground – 'dust to dust'.

2. *A life* (v. 7b). 'God . . . breathed into his nostrils the breath of life and man became a living being.' (The man on the ground 'comes to life'.)

3. *A home* (vv. 8–9 – quote or explain). Eden means a place of delight with its plants and fruit. Earth is home – even for astronauts!

Explain that everything that has been considered so far would be true of animals. They need, and God has given them, bodies, life and a home. However, God has given man, but not animals:

4. *Choice* (vv. 9, 16–17 – quote). Reveal sign-post and get the man to look at it and seem puzzled. Explain that this is the reason why the Bible says that man has been made in the image of God. He is a moral being who can choose between right and wrong.

5. *Culture* (vv. 9–14 – quote or summarise). Speak about the beauty in the garden. Man has been made to enjoy art (show picture) and music (pick up musical instrument and ask organist to play at this point). Perhaps explain that our dogs are not interested in the TV unless a dog barks.

6. *Work* (v. 15 – quote). Reveal garden fork and explain that God has a special purpose for man. Man is happiest when engaged in satisfying work, which is why it is so tragic when much modern industrial work is so boring and many people cannot get work at all. Work was purposeful and pleasant in Eden and will be in heaven.

7. *A wife* (v. 18 – quote). Man is essentially a social creature, but found no real companion among the animals. Just as Adam was specially made, so was Eve specially made for him, not to be his slave, but his companion.

That is what God originally gave man, but Christians know God gave us much more. Enlarge on John 3:16 briefly.

41. David and Bathsheba

Aim

This is one of the expanded outlines referred to in the chapter 'Preaching at All-Age Services'. After reading the passage through more than once it seemed clear that the message in a nutshell was, 'Be sure your sin will find you out.' I jotted down, 'God sees sin, God hates sin, God forgives sin.'

I observed that God has not only ordained scientific laws for the well-being of his universe, but also moral laws that cannot be flouted without serious consequences. It was not for nothing that we have been given the Ten Commandments.

After reading the commentaries on the passage I noted that the story has been repeated day in and day out throughout history and that there were frequent references to Psalms 32 and 51.

A story told in the media at the time was of a well-known personality who had become a Christian and who had admitted to his son he had 'fiddled' his income tax. His son had responded by admitting he regularly stole sweets from a local shop.

I became increasingly convinced that the most valuable material was the story itself, despite the length, but that it contained within it a separate story, namely Nathan's parable, which probably required a different treatment.

I considered using children or young people to do a dramatic presentation, but rejected it because of the delicate nature of the incident. But in any case the speed of the story was important if attention was to be maintained, and the message needed to be applied as the narrative moved, not simply tacked on at the end. If anyone was to tell the story it should be me, so how could I dramatise the different characters? I reduced these to three: King David, husband Uriah and prophet Nathan. (In the context of an all-age service the less said about Bathsheba the better!)

Text

2 Samuel 11–12.

Drama

The talk involves some dramatic action. If further drama is required see *50 Sketches for All Occasions* 22 'Lead Us Not Into . . .'.

Hymns and songs

'He was pierced for our transgressions' (SOF 173); 'Purify my heart' (SOF 475); 'How deep the Father's love for us' (SOF 780).

Prayers

400 Prayers 77, 80–85; Litanies of Confession 101–107.

Main talk

Preparation

I produced three different pieces of headgear to represent the three men: a crown for the king, a close fitting cap for Uriah and a piece of coloured weave kept on with a rope band for the prophet.

For Nathan's parable I made some black line drawings on day-glo paper similar to those in the *Good News Bible* drawn by Annie Vallotton. I stuck Velcro on the back for use on my Teazlegraph board.

I also put Velcro on the back of two pieces of card made to look like tables of stone and on the back of the words *God* and *sin*. I cut out a red cross which could be placed across the word *sin* without making it impossible to read. I put the three words *hates*, *forgives*, *sees* in day-glo letters on Teazlegraph strips to go on the Teazlegraph board.

Finally I had a small table lamp to hand which could actually be switched on, and a wine bottle. I went over the story several times telling it aloud to myself till I felt more or less word perfect.

Presentation

I produced the table lamp and switched it on. I then removed the bulb and asked for volunteers to come and put their fingers on the electric terminus, but of course got none. I then replaced the bulb, so that everything was safe again.

'But God loves you. Would he allow the electricity to harm you?' I asked. By the nodding of heads it was clear everyone thought he would. 'Yes, of course it could kill you!'

'What other laws has God made, apart from scientific ones?'

Someone replied, 'The Ten Commandments.'

'Yes, the moral laws.'

I put the two 'tables' on the Teazlegraph board, one on each side, and also *God* on the left, *sin* on the right and *hates* centred, but a little higher than *God* and *sin*.

I then told the story of David, Bathsheba and Uriah as vividly as I could wearing the crown when quoting David and the small hat when quoting Uriah. I also held the bottle when Uriah was drunk.

I then asked the congregation if they thought God knew

about David's sin. They thought so and I added the word *sees* to the Teazlegraph board centrally but lower than *God* and *sin*, leaving enough space between *hates* and *sees* for the third word in the middle.

I then introduced Nathan the prophet who had obviously come to know what David had done and knew he must tell him he was wrong. The problem was that as David was king he was also the judge of the people and could even judge Nathan.

I explained how Nathan eventually went to the king and told him a story, which I then told, illustrating it with the pictures from the Bible. I asked the congregation why he told that story, and soon had it explained to me. I completed the conversation between David and Nathan and added *forgives* to the Teazlegraph board, explaining that God could do so because he knew Jesus would eventually die for David's sin, as he has for ours. I placed the cross across the word *sin*. I also made brief reference to parts of Psalms 51 and 32.

Finally, I reminded the congregation of a story in the media at that time about a father who 'fiddled' his income tax forms and his son who stole sweets. God knew, and because they had confessed, God forgave. I told everyone that God knew all about them and their sins, and asked them if they had confessed and whether they knew they were forgiven.

42. Matthew Levi

Aim

To draw out some important lessons from the life of this most unlikely disciple of Jesus.

Text

Matthew 9:9–13.

Drama

50 Sketches for All Occasions 25 'An Offer You Can't Refuse'.

Hymns and songs

'God forgave my sin' (SOF 129); 'I believe in Jesus' (SOF 203); 'No eye has seen' (SOF 943).

Prayers

400 Prayers 264–270, 391; Collect for Matthew's Day (CW p. 513).

Main talk

Preparation
Make four large cards having on them the letters L E V I.

Presentation

Warn the congregation that you are going to be using four letter words today! Ask four children to come out to the front and give each of them the letters to spell LEVI.

Ask who has heard of the man in the New Testament who has this name. Mention that Matthew occurs in all lists of the apostles of Jesus, but in Mark's and Luke's Gospels he is referred to as Levi. Only Matthew refers to himself as a tax collector. Since they were regarded as Jewish traitors they were hated and despised, but out of kindness Mark and Luke avoid mentioning Matthew's profession.

Matthew and Jesus both lived in Capernaum, which was an important trade route, and custom house officers, like Matthew, would have had their hands full. It is more than likely that Jesus and Matthew knew each other quite well.

Ask if the congregation think Levi was a good man. On discovering that he wasn't get the child holding the L to move to the other end, so as to spell: E V I L. Refer to the fact that tax collectors in those days always took more than they should. Money ruled Levi's life and Jesus taught 'You cannot serve both God and Money' (Matthew 6:24). But then Jesus also taught that we are all evil (Luke 11:13). It is because of this that we need the gospel, one version of which Matthew Levi was to write. But he was more than just evil. He was also: V I L E. Get children to move to spell that word.

As we have seen, he was not just dishonest but also a traitor. It is all the more surprising, therefore, that Jesus called him, and that he should follow, though he cannot have enjoyed the loneliness and unpopularity of his job. But then God often calls the worst – like Saul of Tarsus, who persecuted Jesus' followers before Jesus called him.

Later, Levi was to write about what Jesus had done for him as a Jew. Get the children to move to spell: V E I L.

Enlarge on the significance of the veil in the Temple being torn in two when Jesus died on the cross.

Lastly get the children to move to spell: L I V E. Matthew Levi was so thrilled to live for Jesus he threw a party. Refer to Matthew 9:10–13. Suggest that we might have been shocked to see the company that Jesus kept. Could we be trusting in our very respectability to earn our place in heaven? We may not be living vile lives, like Matthew, but God sees us all as evil, and so just as much in need of a Saviour as he was.

43. John Mark

Aim

To discover what we can learn from the life of John Mark as revealed in various parts of the New Testament.

Texts

Acts 12:12; 13:13; 2 Timothy 4:11; 1 Peter 5:13.

Hymns and songs

'Father God, I wonder' (SOF 92); 'Praise God for the body' (SOF 461); 'We shall stand' (SOF 589).

Prayers

400 Prayers 389; Collect appointed for St Mark's Day (CW p. 504).

Main talk

Preparation

If possible, obtain props and clothing as used by Sherlock Holmes, eg deer-stalker hat, cloak with cape (I borrowed one from the local theatre for a small fee), a magnifying glass and a pipe. The last I made out of cardboard as I couldn't find the right kind of curved pipe.

Also prepare four cards bent in half. On the inside

have the four texts above written boldly, one on each. On the outside of the card have *CLUE A, B* etc. These should be given secretly to four children before the service begins.

Prepare material for the Teazlegraph board – *John Mark, Kolobo-Dactylus*. Other words: *Christian homes, Useful disciple, Writer*. Pictures of a cross, praying hands, a modern house, a ship with single sail, four symbolic people (ie in different colours) and arrows and two people poring over scrolls. The word *Gospel* on an open book and a hand where the little finger can be pulled away. (Adapt if using OHP.)

Presentation

How many of you like reading detective stories? A famous archbishop said he enjoyed them, providing the body turned up in the first chapter.

We are going to do some detective work this morning so we had better be dressed for the part. (Put on detective outfit.)

We are going to discover all we can about *Kolobo-Dactylus!* Who knows who that might be? (Put word in middle of Teazlegraph board.) Well, I will tell you why he was called that later. His other name was *John Mark*. (Put at top of Teazlegraph board.)

Now what can we discover about him? Perhaps from his Gospel? No, that's no use because there's nothing about the author there. It begins, 'The beginning of the gospel about Jesus Christ the Son of God.' The writer was more interested in Jesus than himself, though I believe Mark does leave his mark! Ask for:

Clue A (Acts 12:12) Get congregation to look it up in their Bibles. Ask what we can learn about Mark's home. Draw out that it was large, hospitable and a praying one. Put on

Teazlegraph board *Christian home* with house and cross and praying hands over it.

I believe this may have been the home where the Lord's Supper was first celebrated. In the excitement typical of Passover time, when Jesus and the disciples sang a hymn and went to the Mount of Olives, Mark followed them and was the young boy mentioned in Mark 14:51–52. If not, who was it and why was it written?

So John Mark came from a happy Christian home. What a privilege. Do we? If so, do we thank God for it?

Clue B (Acts 13:13) Tell the sad story of the first missionary journey and how John Mark returned home before it was finished. (Put up the ship with two men going in one direction – ie Paul and Barnabas – and another, John Mark, going in the other: arrows indicating direction.) Look up Acts 15:36–39 and show how Mark's desertion caused a split and quarrel between Paul and Barnabas. (Put up *Kolobo-Dactylus.*) In the Roman army a deserter would have had his little finger chopped off. So Mark was nicknamed *Kolobo-Dactylus* meaning 'maimed in the finger'. (Put up hand and remove finger.)

Clue C (2 Timothy 4:11 and put up on Teazlegraph board *Useful disciple*) Mark may have deserted, but he came back and was obviously forgiven and became very useful to Paul in the latter days of his ministry in prison. (Put up the remaining figure, preferably in bright yellow.)

Clue D (1 Peter 5:13) 'My son Mark.' Why *son*? Perhaps Peter led him to Jesus in his home. He also helped Peter write a gospel which has lots about Peter in it, including his faults.

Well, what would be our verdict on John Mark? Would we be proud to have his record? He may have had failings but he came back to the Lord and helped Barnabas on the mission

field, assisted Paul in prison and helped Peter write a gospel.
Put up *Gospel-writer* and two men with scrolls.

> We are writing a gospel, a chapter each day,
> In all that we do and in all that we say.
> People read what we write, whether faithless or true.
> Pray, what is the gospel according to you?

44. Stephen

Aim

To tell the story of the first Christian martyr.

Text

Acts 6.

Hymns and songs

'I want to serve the purpose of God' (SOF 260); 'More love, more power' (SOF 392); 'I will offer up my life' (SOF 851).

Prayers

400 Prayers 245; Collect for Stephen's Day (CW p. 443).

Main talk

Preparation

Have the following words either on Teazle-covered cards for use on a Teazlegraph board or on acetate strips to be used on an OHP: *Stephen, He served, He spoke, He suffered.* Cut out from gold paper or card a small crown and put Velcro on the back. (If using OHP have a strip of acetate with a crown on it.)

Presentation

If you are giving this talk on the day after Christmas then you could ask the congregation if they know what day it is, and perhaps make reference to the carol 'Good King Wenceslas'. Put up, not quite at the top of the board, the name *Stephen*. There are just three brief things I want to mention about this great man. (Put up the words as you come to them.)

1. *He served* Explain about the widows getting neglected and there being no state social security provision. Stephen was appointed as one of the seven deacons to deal with the problem. Some people think that the only use they can be in the church is to hand out hymn books or count the collection. Someone has to do those jobs, but there are a whole range of other ways in which Christians can serve in the church as well.

2. *He spoke* Refer to Acts 6:10 and the defence Stephen made in chapter 7. All of us may be called upon to defend our faith at some time or other. Stephen was appalled at the way the temple was worshipped at the expense of God himself. He aimed to show that God did not dwell in houses made with hands. The points he made were that Abraham, Isaac and Israel were nomads; Moses built the tabernacle, but there was no place for God in it; David was prevented from building the temple, and though Solomon his son did, it was second best and Solomon himself acknowledged God had no specific place in it.

Today we can be in danger of idolising church and cathedral buildings as if God had a reserved seat in them. Perhaps tell the story of the boy who was taken to church by his mother for the first time. Mystified by the extraordinary building he tried to ask questions, but was told to be quiet.

On asking why he should keep quiet he was told he was in God's house. 'Well, if I was God I'd move!' was his reply. God is surely in our church building, but then he is every-where, and especially where two or three are gathered in his name.

3. *He suffered* Mention that there are various similarities between Stephen's death and that of the Master whom he served: the blasphemy charge, the illegality of the whole event, the forgiving of the murderers, the committing of the life into the hands of God/Jesus. We might be tempted to say, 'What a waste!' No, for as a result the gospel spread and the greatest Christian missionary the church has ever had was obviously considerably influenced – Saul of Tarsus, who became Paul the apostle.

Jesus said to the church at Smyrna, 'Be faithful unto death, and I will give you the crown of life' (Revelation 2:10). Stephen lived up to his name, for it means crown. Place the visual of the crown over Stephen's name at the top of your board or acetate.

45. Philip and the Ethiopian Treasurer

Aim

To tell the story of Philip the Evangelist's encounter with the Ethiopian treasurer and the subsequent baptism. (The talk is particularly suitable for an Anglican baptism service.)

Text

Acts 8:26–40, read from *The Dramatised Bible*.

Hymns and songs

'One shall tell another' (SOF 439); 'When I feel the touch' (SOF 594); 'Jesus Christ' (SOF 865); 'Speak, Lord' (HTC 510).

Prayers

Church Family Worship, Section 6, 'At a baptism'; Holy Baptism Service (CW p. 344).

Main talk

Preparation

Prepare twelve small pictures on an acetate as follows:

First set: The child and the chemist
1. A small child crying
2. A doctor examining the child

182

3. The chemist handing over medicine to the child's mother
4. The child smiling

Second set: Spiritual sickness and cure
5. A man with the word 'sinner' printed on him
6. A Bible
7. A church
8. A cross

Third set: Baptism and faith
9. A tiny baby screaming
10. A family with the mother holding the baby
11. A Sunday school class
12. A bishop laying hands on someone's head in a confirmation service

The first four pictures should be fixed across the top of the acetate and the last four fixed to the bottom. The middle four should be fixed so that 'sin' and 'the Bible' are both on the left, with the latter covering the former, and 'the church' and 'the cross' are both on the right, with latter covering the former.

Presentation

1. *The child and the chemist* Show the first picture. Ask what might be wrong with the child. Suppose it is tummy-ache? What can the mother do? Talk about going to the doctor (second picture), taking the prescription to the chemist and getting medicine (third picture), and taking the medicine and feeling better (fourth picture).

2. *Spiritual sickness and cure* We are all sinners and need to find a cure (see Romans 3:23 and 6:23). Show the fifth picture. Ask where the Ethiopian eventually found a solution to his problem (show sixth picture). Who helped him

understand it? Philip – who in this case represented the church (show seventh picture). Did the Ethiopian eat the scroll of Isaiah? No. Just as the child did not eat the paper the prescription was written on. But as the prescription led to the medicine, so the Bible passage led to Jesus and what he did on the cross (show eighth picture). Talk about Isaiah 53 and the need to believe.

3. *Baptism and faith* Small babies have not sinned, but it soon becomes clear they are born sinners and show it (show ninth picture). They need to be brought up in a family that reads the Bible and prays (show tenth picture). They should be brought to church, where they will be helped to understand the Bible and come to faith in Jesus Christ (show eleventh picture). When old enough they should testify to being Christians by confirming the baptismal vows that were taken for them when they were babies (show twelfth picture).

46. Blinded: Saul of Tarsus

Aim

To tell the story of the conversion of Saul of Tarsus and its application to us.

Text

Acts 9:1–22.

Drama

50 Sketches for All Occasions 24 'Home Improvements'. Also Scripture Union soundstrip or video *On Fire* part 5 'Blinded'. If a video can be easily shown in church, then part of the Scripture Union video *All or Nothing* might be shown.

Hymns and songs

'Give me, Lord, a dream from heaven' (SOF 727); 'Lord, I come to You' (SOF 895); 'Thank You for saving me' (SOF 1015).

Prayers

400 Prayers 245, 367; Collect for Conversion of Paul (CW p. 500).

Main talk

Preparation

Have the following three words, with accompanying simple visuals, either on OHP acetates or on cards that could be held up or placed on a Teazlegraph board:

VISION – with a picture of an eye
VOICE – with a picture of lips
VERDICT – with a picture of a T-junction road sign

Presentation

Our story is one of the most important and well authenticated events in the Bible, second only to the passion and resurrection of Jesus. Luke tells the story three times (Acts 9, 22, 26).

Ask who the first Christian martyr was. Saul saw Stephen die and was probably privately very impressed.

Refer to the journey to Damascus from Jerusalem, which is about 150 miles, and would have taken several days, giving plenty of time for Saul to reflect on what the Christians were preaching, comparing it with the message of the Old Testament, which he would have known well.

Note that according to Acts 26:13 Saul was reaching Damascus about midday, so that the sun, shining on light baked earth, could be physically blinding in any case, but that does not rule out a supernatural light as well.

1. *The vision* Ask what Saul saw. Probably a supernatural light. Tell the story of the Indian, Sundar Singh, who, like Saul, was initially bitterly opposed to the gospel. However, praying one early morning, he saw a great light:

Then, as I prayed and looked into the light, I saw the form of the Lord Jesus Christ. It had such an appearance of glory and love. If it had been some Hindu incarnation I would have prostrated myself before it. But it was the Lord Jesus Christ whom I had been insulting a few days before. I felt a vision like this could not come out of my own imagination.

2. *The voice* Ask what Saul heard. Sundar Singh's experience was similar:

> I heard a voice saying in Hindustani: 'How long will you perse-cute me? I have come to save you. You were praying to know the right way; why do you not take it?'

The man who was to become the great bishop of the church, St Augustine of Hippo (AD 354–430), led a very sinful life as a young man. But he tells in his *Confessions*:

> I heard a voice, as if it had been some boy or girl from a house not far off, uttering and often repeating in a sing-song manner, 'Take up and read, take up and read.'

This led directly to him picking up a Bible, opening it and reading where it fell open at Romans 13:13–14:

> Let us behave decently, as in the daytime, not in orgies and drunkenness . . . Rather, clothe yourselves with the Lord Jesus Christ, and do not think about how to gratify the desires of the sinful nature.

3. *The verdict* Saul realised that Jesus had risen from the dead, as the Christians had been preaching, and everything else fell into place. He must now become a preacher of the same message.

Sundar Singh came to the same conclusion:

> Jesus Christ is not dead but living and it must be he himself. So I fell at his feet and got this wonderful peace which I could not get anywhere else. This is the joy I was wishing to get. When I

got up, the vision had all disappeared, but . . . the peace and joy
have remained with me ever since.

(Note that there is no evidence that Sundar had ever heard
the story of St Paul's conversion.)

C. S. Lewis, author of the Narnia books, says in his auto-
biography:

> You must picture me alone in that room at Magdalen, night
> after night, feeling, whenever my mind lifted even for a second
> from my work, the steady, unrelenting approach of Him whom
> I so earnestly desired not to meet. That which I greatly feared
> had at last come upon me. In the Trinity Term of 1929 I gave in,
> and admitted that God was God, and knelt and prayed:
> perhaps, that night, the most dejected and reluctant convert in
> all England. I did not then seen what is now the most shining
> and obvious thing; the Divine humility which will accept a
> convert even on such terms. The Prodigal Son at least walked
> home on his own two feet. But who can but adore that Love
> which will open the high gates to a prodigal who is brought in
> kicking, struggling, resentful, and darting his eyes in every
> direction for a chance of escape? (*Surprised by Joy*,
> HarperCollins)

End with some sort of brief appeal to those who have not
reached the same verdict as Saul, Sundar, Augustine and
C. S. Lewis.

47. Timothy: Man of God

Aim

To discover all we can about the Christian life as revealed in the life of Timothy. This talk could be used on Mothering Sunday.

Text

2 Timothy 1:1–7; 2:1–7; 3:14–17.

Drama

Acting Up 'Friends', pp. 68–70; *50 Sketches for All Occasions* 17 'The Trip of a Lifetime'.

Hymns and songs

'Be bold, be strong' (SOF 37); 'For the joys and for the sorrows' (SOF 721); 'We are marching in the light of God' (SOF 1076).

Prayers

400 Prayers 68, 196, 200, 201.

Main talk

Preparation

Prepare for use on a Teazlegraph board the following words (with suggested colours in day-glo card) or adapt for OHP:

> *TIMOTHY, shy, sick* (green)
> *MAN of GOD, brave, loyal* (red)
> *home* (pink), *Scriptures* (white)
> *friendship* (buff), *Spirit* (red and orange alternately)
> *effort* (yellow)

Prepare also the following drawings after the style of the line figures in the *Good News Bible* by Annie Vallotton: a sickly boy (green), a cross and soldier (red), a mother in attitude of prayer (pink), a scroll, two people greeting each other (buff) flames (in red and orange), an athlete (yellow). Also take a cover of, say, a *Good News Bible* and stick Velcro on the back.

The way all these visual aids are arranged on the Teazlegraph board will depend on its size. In any case the whole plan should be worked out carefully beforehand and everything taken off and filed in the order that the items will be required. I would suggest that the green and red items are shown on one side of your board and the remainder on the reverse side. In the presentation which follows, the visual aids are in italics when they should be placed on the board.

Presentation

We who are parents, what do we really want for our children? To be happy? Of course, but how? A secure job, adequate money and successful marriage – these may all help towards a happy life.

I want to suggest a worthier aim – that they become men

and women of God. This may possibly sound dull, but if Jesus promised us the abundant life (John 10:10) then surely it should be the best and happiest life.

Let's see how this worked out in the life of one biblical character.

TIMOTHY (Place top of board)
Humanly speaking he was a timid, *shy* boy, not naturally very courageous, rather easily tempted, perhaps easily led. He was prone to illness, especially tummy-ache (put up *sick*). He was brought up in Lystra in Asia Minor, his mother being a Jewess who taught him the Old Testament, probably helped by his grandmother. His father was a Greek. Timothy became a . . .

MAN of GOD (Place to right of board)
How did the change come about? Talk about the apostle Paul's visit on his first missionary journey, as a result of which Timothy, his mother and grandmother all became Christians. (Put up *cross* on right of the boy and words *shy* and *sick*.)

Later, on his second missionary journey, Paul called at Lystra and received a very good report of Timothy, so took him with him. Timothy became a minister and *soldier* of Jesus Christ.

Refer to his bravery in service with Paul and Silas (put up *brave*). Later Paul wrote to the Philippians: 'He is the only one who shares my feelings and who really cares about you. . . . He has proved his worth,' (Philippians 2:20–22 GNB). (Put up *loyal*.)

At the end of Paul's life, when he was in prison and expecting death, he wrote: 'Do your best to come to me soon.' So Timothy, shy and sick, became the brave, loyal successor of the greatest Christian missionary of all time.

What was the secret? (Reverse Teazlegraph board)

In one sense the single answer is that Timothy became a Christian. But that needs unpacking. Suggest and briefly comment on the following factors and apply to congregation.

(a) *Home* (put up *praying woman*). Refer to mother's prayers and example.

(b) *Scriptures* (put up *scroll* and Bible cover). Quote from 2 Timothy 3:15–17. Timothy probably wrote down at least three of Paul's letters and two were sent to him. He would have heard much of the Old Testament from his mother.

(c) *Friendship* (put up *two people greeting*). Paul and Timothy were deeply attached to each other (2 Timothy 1:4). Stress the importance of the right friends.

(d) *Spirit* (put up *flames*). Refer to the gift of God (2 Timothy 1:6–7). The Holy Spirit is several times referred to as a fire that must not be quenched but rekindled.

(e) *Effort* (put up athlete). Refer to 2 Timothy 2:5 and Philippians 2:12b–13. All the things we have been thinking about – the influence of home, Scriptures, friends and the Holy Spirit – will be useless unless we co-operate and this will mean effort. So may we all enjoy the abundant life of men and women of God.

48. Invitation Talk

Aim

A general gospel talk on some of the excuses people make for refusing God's invitation.

Text

Luke 14:15–24.

Drama

50 Sketches for All Occasions 50 'The Invitation'.

Hymns and songs

'Come and see' (SOF 67); 'Here is love' (SOF 168); 'Come let us worship Jesus' (SOF 692); 'I am trusting you, Lord Jesus' (HTC 433); 'Just as I am, without one plea' (HTC 440).

Prayers

400 Prayers (confession of sin) 81–85, (faith) 3, 46, 72, 202.

Main talk

Preparation

Construct a large envelope with the following words on the front:

A SINNER
LOST LANE
EARTH

Draw a postmark with *Heaven* on it and *33 AD* in the middle. Draw a red stamp with a lamb on it and other marks to suggest the crucifixion. Mark over the stamp franked wavy lines. Inside the envelope put a card with an invitation:

God says
Come to my supper
RSVP

Make a door with a letter box out of a large piece of cardboard. Assemble props for drama as mentioned in the presentation. Perhaps you can borrow a postman's uniform and have someone dressed up and hidden from view.

Prepare the scene for the drama which follows.

Presentation

Ask who likes going to parties, and make traditional references if it is near Christmas. Explain that you have got an invitation to a party. (The postman appears with the envelope at this point.) Ask to whom it is addressed. Upon receiving the reply 'A Sinner' ask who that is. Draw out that it means every single one of us on this earth. Because we are sinners we live in 'Lost Lane'.

Ask who the invitation is from. Suggest that a child comes up to see the postmark, which will be too small to be seen at a distance. Explain that this invitation is from God, and that he especially issued the invitation around 33 AD.

Ask someone to suggest what happened that year. Draw out the answer that Jesus died. Enquire who pays to send an invitation by post. (Answer: 'the sender'.) It costs God to send this invitation.

Examine the stamp, which has a picture of the Lamb of God and other symbols suggesting the crucifixion, explaining briefly what it means. Now produce the invitation from the envelope and read the words on it. Ask what RSVP means. Draw out that we have to reply.

Will everyone want to say 'Yes'? Most people want to go to parties, but the extraordinary thing is, as Jesus pointed out in a story he told, most people refuse God's supper for various reasons. Here are some excuses they might give.

Scene 1
(Set the scene with a small sofa placed near the front. Arrange for two responsible older children to hold up the door with the letter box in it. They move left of stage and as they do so the postman puts a letter through the letter box.)

Enter First Boy and Girl, both dressed in jeans, boy carrying saw and wood, girl carrying paint pot and wallpaper. They move to door and girl picks up letter and reads it.

FIRST GIRL: Old money-bags up at mansion wants us to go to have a nosh-up with 'im!

FIRST BOY: What's 'e up to? Wants to show off 'is new 'ouse, I bet!

FIRST GIRL: Oh Dan – it'd be exciting!

FIRST BOY: OK, so what! We'll never get this 'ouse done unless we get on with it, and we've got the Joneses coming next week. Yer'd better think of an excuse. *(Both go off.)*

Scene 2
Children move door to centre and receive another letter from postman.

(Second Boy and Girl appear, well dressed. He picks up the letter and reads.)

SECOND BOY: Samantha, His Lordship wants us to dine with him next Sunday.

SECOND GIRL: George, we can't! We're driving over to the Lakes then, to try out the new car – you promised!

SECOND BOY: Don't worry, darling. I haven't forgotten. I'll tell him I must test the car and that is the only day I've got.

Scene 3
Children move door to right of stage and receive third letter from postman. Third Boy and Girl appear holding hands. Boy sits down on sofa and girl picks up letter and looks at envelope.

THIRD GIRL: Mr *and Mrs* John Smith! (*she quickly opens up and reads*) J. B. wants us to go over to his place on the 19th (*pause*) – that will be your first night off since our honeymoon.

THIRD BOY: Don't worry, precious, we'll think of something. You're not for sharing – not yet, anyway!
                (*They cuddle on the sofa, lights dim.*)
                (*Children holding door and Third Boy and Girl move off.*)

End with an appeal for some in the congregation to stop making excuses for not accepting God's invitation to make Christ Saviour and Lord.

49. The Good Samaritan

Aim

To teach that the gospel of God's love for us in Christ must have an outward response in our love for our neighbour.

Text

Luke 10:25–37.

Drama

Acting Up 'The Samaritan Rap', pp. 27–29; *50 Sketches for All Occasions* 33 'Love is . . .'.

Hymns and songs

'A new commandment' (SOF 22); 'Beauty for brokenness' (SOF 664); 'Give me a heart of compassion' (SOF 726).

Prayers

400 Prayers 63, 67, 145, 172, 218, 240, 274, 299.

Main talk

Preparation

Though this talk was written for a specific and unique occasion it could easily be adapted for any occasion when the social implications of the gospel need to be taught. The visuals for the talk were all painted by an artist in the congregation for use on the Teazlegraph board. The background at the top right-hand corner of the picture which includes heaven is Leeds, where the Crypt is situated. Velcro was stuck on the backs of all the visuals. These can easily be adapted if OHP is being used.

Presentation

A clever lawyer (at least he thought he was clever) was trying to catch Jesus out with a religious question: 'How do you get to heaven?' Of course he thought he knew all the possible answers Jesus could give. Jesus simply asked him what was written in the Bible (our Old Testament). The lawyer was really embarrassed by that, for Jesus was treating him like a child.

He blurts out the two great commandments on loving God and neighbour. 'That's right,' says Jesus. 'Do that and you'll get to heaven.'

Sounds easy enough, but the lawyer cannot let Jesus have the last word, so he asks who his neighbour is. Jesus replies with one of his best known stories, the Good Samaritan. Tell the story in your own words, putting up the visuals at the appropriate moments.

Modern application We are all on a journey. (Reverse the board and put up *heaven* and the other visuals as you refer to them.) Like the lawyer we want to know how to get to heaven. But like the route to Jericho the journey is hazardous. Special perils in the city are unemployment, gambling and drink, which can leave us half dead.

Along comes the *gospel preacher* on his way to a great conference to tell people about the love of God and how Jesus came to save sinners. Such people know they must get their priorities right. Too many people have just a social gospel. He passes by on the other side.

Then along comes an *average church member*. He thinks to himself that he does plenty for the church, and there are others to look after tramps. He, too, passes by on the other side.

Finally along comes the modern *Good Samaritan*. His background is a bit uncertain, and one cannot be quite sure his beliefs are entirely orthodox. However, he goes over to the man on the ground, loves and cares for him and gets him all the help he needs.

The talk could be concluded with the story of Bill, as told by Rebecca Manley Pippert in *Out of the Saltshaker* (IVP) pp. 177–8.

50. Biblical Fools

Aim

To examine the theme of foolishness in the Bible. A talk that might be suitable for use near April Fool's Day.

Texts

Psalm 14:1; Luke 12:20; 1 Corinthians 4:10.

Drama

50 Sketches for All Occasions 42 'The Rich Fool'; *Scenes and Wonders* 'A Bag of Happiness' pp. 8–11.

Hymns and songs

'I lift my eyes up' (SOF 221); 'We believe' (SOF 572); 'You have taken the precious' (SOF 1138).

Prayers

400 Prayers 217, 240.

Main talk

Preparation

Prepare pictures as shown below. The man on the left is the Psalmist, the man in the centre is the Rich Fool of Jesus' parable in Luke 12, and the man on the right is the 'Fool for Christ's sake'. Each visual should have Velcro on the back for use on the Teazlegraph board. Adapt if using OHP.

Presentation

I want to introduce you to three fools referred to in the Bible and to ask which one most fits you.

1. *The fool who said there was no God* Refer to Psalm 14 and put up the Psalmist on the board. The Psalmist was really saying that some said 'God does not matter', but what they really meant was 'Sin does not matter'. Explain that sin obviously does matter very much because of two things. *Conscience*: why were we given this moral regulator if sin is unimportant? *The cross of Christ*: why did Jesus die on the cross if sin doesn't matter? Do you say sin doesn't matter because God does not matter? If so, the Bible calls you a fool.

2. *The rich fool* Tell the story of the Rich Fool in Luke 12 in your own words, putting up the visuals as they become relevant. Most people would call the man a very able administrator and anything but a fool. But God saw that his life was just concerned with himself, his money, his pleasure, whereas Jesus came to bring abundant life, eternal life, a new quality of life that never ends, so he was foolishly missing the best.

The other reason why he was a fool was because he forgot that he did not know how long was his life. Refer to someone known to the congregation who has recently died unexpectedly and young. When the rich man died, his wealth was no use to him. Someone once asked, on hearing that a millionnaire had died, how much he had left, to which the answer was given 'Everything'.

Are you just living for yourself and this life, with no thought for God and eternity? Then God calls you a fool.

3. *The wise fool* Quote 1 Corinthians 4:10. (Put up the clown.) Refer to the musical *Godspell* which shocked some people, because the clown represented Jesus. In one sense what a foolish life he lived. He lived totally for other people, never giving any thought for himself; he made no attempt to seek high office, never got married, settled down or reared a family. Knowing perfectly well the religious leaders were plotting his murder he walked straight into their trap and refused to defend himself when on trial. The religious leaders called him mad, yet he challenged the world to follow him, and millions down the centuries have done so and found abundant life as a consequence – like the apostle Paul, who admitted he was a fool for Christ's sake.

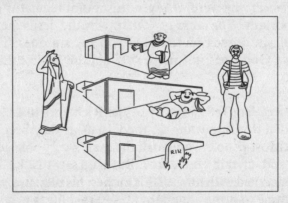

How does such a foolish life begin? Refer to 1 Corinthians 1:18 and explain briefly about the cross. Those who follow Jesus will be seen as foolish in the world's eyes. At baptism we are told not to be ashamed to be Christ's soldiers and servants. End with the story of the hot-gospeller who wore sandwich boards. On one side was 'A fool for Christ's sake'. But when people turned round to see what was on his back they read 'Whose fool are you?'

Subject Index

Scripture Index

50 Sketches for all Occasions

by Michael Botting

A rich collection of sketches from a variety of sources – including teachers, ministers, drama group leaders and theatre companies – to provide something for almost any occasion.

Whether you are looking to liven up your Christmas or Easter services, provide an opportunity for outreach, or simply illustrate a talk, this resource with its index of themes and Scripture references is sure to help.

If you have never used drama before, the introductory section provides vital clues to all you need to know, including:

- visibility and audibility
- basic mime techniques
- the use of minimal props and equipment
- involving children

400 Prayers for Church, Home and School

by Michael Botting

This collection of prayers comes out of years of experience with family services in different churches, but equally importantly the experience of parenthood and of leading school assemblies.

The prayers are arranged under festivals and seasons, subjects and themes, and the school section covers both primary and secondary age groups.

Whether you are helping to lead a church service, a school assembly, or a family prayer time at home, this book will provide a rich resource – one you will want to return to time and again.

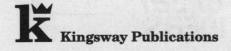

Kingsway Publications